How to write Genre Flash Fiction

Historical, Romance, Fantasy, Science Fiction, Horror and Thriller

Sally Dickson

Typeset in Atticus

Printed and bound in Great Britain by Ingram Spark part of Lightning Source UK Ltd

Lightning Source UK Ltd is committed to improving environmental performance by driving down CO2 emissions and reducing, reusing and recycling waste.
Lightning Source UK Ltd recognizes that what we do today, affects the environment of both current and future generations and we are therefore committed to continuous environmental improvement. Our policy is to manage our businesses in such a manner as to have minimum impact on the environment in which we operate.

Book Cover and illustrations by Sally Dickson
1st edition, 2024

CONTENTS

INTRODUCTION

WHY I DECIDED TO WRITE THIS BOOK.

THERE ARE NOT MANY books written about genre fiction—romance, historical fiction, fantasy, science fiction, horror, and thrillers. These genres are often overlooked in favour of literary fiction.

Oh, and the applause from the gallery when a literary author dips their toe into the genre category!

I read everything—back of cereal packs, flyers, blogs, novels, Booker Prize-winning books, newspapers, academic papers, and science fiction. And I believe, whisper it, as a book lover, you have the most fun when reading genre fiction.

The unashamed action and adventure, the lifelong torturous loves, the death, cheating, revenges, the chases, the fights, the spills, the sex, the gore, and the death.

Great genre fiction takes you by the hand and yanks you into a world of its own making, where, as a reader, you can lose yourself for an hour, a day, or in the case of a series, several weeks—or indeed a lifetime.

As a writer and judge of short-short story contests (the Farnham Flash Fiction Competition is now in its 7th year and has had over 1,000 entries), let me tell you a secret: In short-short story contests, genre fiction entries are in the minority. And don't get me wrong, it's complicated to get genre fiction to work in 500 words or fewer. But when it does work, it's spellbinding. Flash fiction at its best normally has a twist in the tale—so violent, so unexpected—it's like a turning car spinning on its axis in a doughnut. Genre fiction is the writing style with the largest number of tools and tricks at its disposal to deliver the most jaw-dropping twists in the tale.

So, I have written this book to set out how genre fiction should work in flash fiction. I offer you guidance on how to world-build in a couple of sentences, details of character types you can fall back on, and common tropes readers know well so that you, as a writer, can subvert them. And, as always, lots of exercises and other plots to motivate your writing.

Let's get started.

750 WORDS: WHAT IS GENRE FICTION?

How to Write Genre Fiction

So, YOU WRITE INTO genre fiction? Historical fiction, romance, fantasy epic, science fiction saga, horror and thrillers. Great job. Excellent choice!

Writing genre fiction is like strapping yourself into a rollercoaster of imagination—expect twists, turns, and the thrill of creating worlds that readers can't wait to lose themselves in.

Unlike literary fiction, which tends to delve into deep character studies, genre fiction is all about embracing the conventions that make each category—whether it's mystery, romance, science fiction, fantasy, horror, or thriller—so irresistibly gripping.

The goal? Craft stories that pull readers into a journey so engaging they forget where they are.

Ready to get started? Let's dive into what makes genre fiction tick.

Understanding Genre Conventions

First things first—know your playground. Each genre has its own rules and expectations.

- In a mystery, there's a crime, a detective, and a trail of clues leading to that satisfying 'aha!' moment.

- Romance? It's all about the sparks between characters, with an ending that leaves hearts warm and fuzzy.

- Both Fantasy and Science fiction by definition see you build entire worlds, layering in futuristic tech or ancient magic so convincing it has to be real.

- Horror is here to make your skin crawl,

- Thrillers keep you on the edge of your seat with high-stakes tension.

Your mission is to soak up these conventions. Read voraciously, study the masters, and understand how they play by the rules—so you can break them like a pro.

Crafting Engaging Plots

Plot is where the magic happens. It's the engine of your story, propelling it from one adrenaline-pumping scene to the next.

In genre fiction, this means understanding the genre's narrative structure.

- Mystery? Plant those clues like breadcrumbs, but don't forget the red herrings.

- Romance? Build that delicious tension and throw in some obstacles to keep the lovers on their toes.

- In sci-fi or fantasy, your plot might revolve around an epic quest or galaxy-shattering conflict.

- And thrillers? Keep that tension dialled up to eleven.

Outlining your plot before you dive in can help keep things on track—though sometimes, the best twists come from letting your characters take the wheel.

Embracing Tropes and Subverting Expectations

Tropes are your best friends in genre fiction—but don't let them get too comfortable. Readers love familiar elements, but they also crave surprises. Embrace those well-worn paths, then veer off them with a twist no one saw coming.

In a romance, maybe the 'boy meets girl' becomes 'girl meets girl' in a futuristic cityscape. Or in a thriller, your protagonist isn't a grizzled PI but a stay-at-home dad suddenly thrust into a life-or-death situation.

The trick is to balance the expected with the unexpected, creating a story that feels both familiar and fresh.

Writing Genre Flash Fiction

In this book, we are going to explore the specific challenges of writing genre flash fiction and short fiction, where you only have 500 to 1,000 words to tell a story.

- To do this well, you need to master three specific skills of genre writing.

- You need to understand the reader's expectations of the genre—the voice, the story arc, and the satisfying outcomes.

- More often than not, you will need to use familiar locations or settings; after all, you don't have many words to create a whole new world.

The real skill lies in the twist—after drawing the reader in with familiar genre storylines and backdrops, you need to find an original twist in the tale. The beauty of writing genre fiction is that you have a vast palette of colours and a wide array of options at your disposal.

When done well, Genre Flash Fiction is the most compelling and memorable short fiction of all.

1000 WORDS. ORIGINALITY IN FLASH FICTION

LET'S FACE IT, IF you choose to write genre flash fiction, it's for one of two reasons:

1. You can't write anything else.

Hands up, that's me. Close my eyes, and its foreign planets and silver ships skimming the upper atmosphere. Nearly all the flash fiction I write is science fiction, horror, or thrillers.

2. You want to be different.

A well-executed genre flash fiction piece will stand out in a crowded flash fiction competition, so it's worth practicing if you'd like to win.

You've chosen genre flash fiction, turning your back on bedroom dramas, kitchen sinks, traumas, funeral sagas, and lonely wives plotting their partners' demise. No, you've opted for a wider canvas. But how do you evoke Middle Earth with its hobbits, elves, wizards, and thousands of horse lords in just 500 words?

The truth is, you can't.

Whether it's romance, historical fiction, science fiction, fantasy, thriller, or horror, you need to walk a tightrope. On one hand, use characters and situations (tropes) the reader quickly understands. Then, you need a brilliant idea (a bright spark) to subvert these tropes and end with a shock or twist.

Know your genre.

If you're like me, you eat, sleep, read, watch science fiction, and repeat. If that's you, then you know your genre. My goal here is to provide you with checklists and descriptions to help you categorize your fiction.

Let's start with a Fantasy.

For instance, in fantasy you might say, I'm writing an epic fantasy quest for a magical unicorn...but after much peril, the gift the unicorn bestows is death (heroic death, peaceful death, or planetary-wide death—you decide!).

So, how do you pull people into this story with tropes they recognize? You might use a band of dwarfs, adding comedic notes through their dialogue and interactions. But then, subvert this well-known trope. Maybe their leader is a woman dwarf in disguise, or the dwarfs are trying to help an injured Elven princess. You could go all action-adventure by adding a volcano, a dragon, or troll-infested mines. Or you could opt for a full-on character study, exploring the dilemmas and sadness driving the dwarfs to act.

Choose a fantasy backdrop: woodland, mountain, volcanic plains, and more. You can have magical trees or whispering birds. The point is, the story must end with finding the unicorn and the revelation that their magic bestows death.

Every choice should recognize: "Okay, I choose this because my reader recognizes it and can easily imagine it, but I add this twist to keep it interesting." Layer as much color and detail as you can through verb and adjective choices. Tweak your dialogue, syntax, and descriptions of clothes, weapons, utensils, and accommodation. Richness is the key to success in genre fiction.

Let's try another. This time a Thriller

I'm writing a James Bond-style action sequence where the protagonist is a woman, and the chase is an escape through Selfridges to buy the perfect gift for her husband. Okay, forget it that's been done before.

Let's try again. I'm writing a James Bond-milk-tray-style hero adventure where the protagonist is a loving wife making her way back to her husband. To add a twist, set the action in Paris or Nice instead of London, Oxford, or New York. If in Paris, imagine a furtive enemy—a gang of urban petty thieves preying on tourists—whom our heroine defeats at every turn. If in Nice, imagine a group of trafficked teenagers selling cheap sunglasses on the beach, whom our heroine rescues and hands over to the correct authorities, all before heading home with Prosecco and cake for her hubby.

With every decision, ask yourself: Is this a common storyline or trope? How can I add a twist to make it different? How can I ratchet it up to make the final twist a proper rollercoaster finish?

In the Paris petty thieves scenario, we could pile up the action so the heroine is stealing from the thieves to get the elements (flowers, wine, and food) for the perfect dinner.

One last example:

I'm writing a romance story about a love triangle. One woman, two men, or one man and two women—you decide.

Next decision: location. What year is it? How old is your protagonist? Mix it up. If you always write about Cambridge, switch to Oxford, York, or Blackpool. Could you write a love triangle set in an end-of-life hospice or at a clinic for the newly blind?

Next decision: When do you set your fiction? All love triangles have a recognizable story arc:

1. Meet partner A.

2. Meet partner B.

3. Realize you like them both.

4. Complications of keeping both your partners apart and happy.

5. The moment you are found out.

6. The aftermath: either they're lonely and miserable, or they form a joyful ménage à trois.

The most potential for compelling flash fiction comes at Step 4 or Step 6—either the comedy of trying to keep two lovers apart yet happy, with the inevitable chaos and confusion that ensues, or the aftermath. You could write a lovely reverie on the past, with the twist being the revelation of one's current situation (the bleaker, the better).

Alternatively, write a joyful glimpse of a happy ménage à trois, with hints at the bumps along the road that brought you there.

The point is to be deliberate—know what you're writing, see it from a distance, analyze and twist it to make the most original flash fiction you can.

Okay, I think I've said enough on originality.

To be really original you need to know the most common storys, story arcs or tropes used by millions of writers in Flash Fiction

600 WORDS: STORY ARCS AND TROPES IN FLASH FICTION

IMPORTANT TO KNOW

To MAKE YOUR FLASH fiction stand out, knowing the most common tropes in genre fiction—whether it's romance, fantasy, historical fiction, horror, science fiction, or thriller—is crucial. Ask yourself, what's the core story here? Has it been told before? If so, what will the reader expect? Then, how can you twist and subvert those expectations?

Let's explore ten of the most common tropes or story arcs in genre fiction, along with examples. Think of a story that matches each description. The real challenge? Finding a way to make these well-worn tropes feel fresh and original.

1. The Star-Crossed Lovers

Description: Two characters from different social classes, cultures, or warring factions fall in love, facing insurmountable odds.

Example: Romeo and Juliet by William Shakespeare.

Twist It: Set the lovers in a dystopian future where their love defies artificial intelligence laws.

2. The Forgotten Hero

Description: A character whose bravery or sacrifice was overlooked by history, often due to their gender, race, or social status.

Example: Hidden Figures by Margot Lee Shetterly.

Twist It: A forgotten hero from an alternate history where women led the Industrial Revolution.

3. The Fish Out of Water

Description: A character from one era or culture is thrust into another, struggling to adapt to the unfamiliar customs.

Example: Outlander by Diana Gabaldon.

Twist It: A medieval knight wakes up in a high-tech, gender-neutral future society.

4. The Noble Outlaw

Description: A character who lives outside the law but is morally upright, often stealing from the rich to help the poor.

Example: Robin Hood by Howard Pyle.

Twist It: A modern-day hacker steals corporate secrets to expose corruption, all while on the run.

5. The Tragic Flaw

Description: A character with a significant flaw that leads to their downfall, set against historical events.

Example: Macbeth by William Shakespeare.

Twist It: A scientist's obsession with immortality during the Victorian era leads to a gruesome end.

6. The Disguised Identity

Description: A character who hides their true identity to escape persecution or achieve a specific goal.

Example: The Scarlet Pimpernel by Baroness Orczy.

Twist It: A WWII spy masquerades as a Nazi officer, risking everything to save lives.

7. The Last Stand

Description: A group of characters making a final, desperate effort to defend their way of life or a cause, often doomed to fail.

Example: The Alamo by John Myers Myers.

Twist It: A band of rebels fights their last stand against an alien invasion in the distant future.

8. The Secret Keeper

Description: A character who holds crucial knowledge or a dangerous secret that could change the course of events.

Example: The Da Vinci Code by Dan Brown.

Twist It: An ancient manuscript hidden in a monastery reveals the truth about a long-forgotten civilization.

9. The Rise from Rags

Description: A character who starts from humble beginnings and rises to power or wealth through cleverness, bravery, or luck.

Example: Oliver Twist by Charles Dickens.

Twist It: A street urchin in a post-apocalyptic world becomes the leader of a resistance movement.

10. The Forbidden Knowledge

Description: A character discovers or seeks out knowledge considered taboo or dangerous by society, often with dire consequences.

Example: Frankenstein by Mary Shelley.

Twist It: In a future where memories are traded as commodities, a hacker uncovers a government conspiracy that could destroy humanity.

These storytelling story arcs and tropes are cherished because they tap into universal themes and emotions. The key is to make them your own, adding twists that surprise and delight your readers.

100 WORDS: AN INTRODUCTION TO HISTORICAL FICTION AS FLASH FICTION

DIGGING UP THE PAST

HISTORICAL FLASH FICTION DRAWS on the rich tapestry of the past, offering writers a unique playground to mix the familiar with the unexpected.

This genre is perfect for flash fiction, providing instantly recognizable settings and events like ancient Rome, Tudor England, or the American Civil War. With a few sharp details, you can transport readers to a specific moment in time, educate, inform, or even subvert common knowledge.

It's all about making history relevant and entertaining, engaging readers with concise, impactful storytelling.

Dive into history and unleash your creativity in the realm of Historical Flash Fiction!

700 WORDS: WRITING HISTORICAL FLASH FICTION

STRATEGIES TO GET IT RIGHT

The Accuracy Balancing Act

YOU GREATEST CHALLENGE IN historical fiction is accuracy. Readers expect the setting, dialogue, and details to be spot-on. You need to know everything—from the clothes people wore to the social customs they observed. But flash fiction doesn't give you the luxury of endless description. So, how do you convey a historically accurate world in just 500 words?

Strategies:

1. Select Key Details:

Focus on a few evocative details that instantly ground the reader in the era. A "clink of coins in a leather pouch" or "the scent of horse-drawn carriages on cobblestone streets" can do wonders without overwhelming your narrative.

2. Embed Research in the Narrative:

Skip the info dumps. Weave historical details into your characters' actions and dialogue. A character's frustration with the slow speed of a mail coach, for example, can highlight the era's main communication methods.

3. Use Period-Appropriate Language:

You don't need lengthy monologues, but the tone and language should reflect the time. Choose words and phrases from the period to avoid anachronisms that nearly always pull readers out of the story.

Context vs. Narrative: Finding the Sweet Spot

So you know, the setting is more than just a backdrop—it shapes the entire story. You have to balance historical context with the need to tell a gripping tale. How do you ensure you're giving enough context without slowing the story?

Strategies:

1. Zoom In on a Specific Moment:

Instead of tackling broad events, focus on a single moment that captures the essence of the era. A conversation between two soldiers during World War I can suggest the broader conflict without further explanation.

2. Imply the Larger World:

Use details to imply the context. A character glancing at a newspaper headline about "unrest in the colonies" gives a sense of the times without spelling it out.

3. Leverage Historical Conflicts or Events:

Use well-known events as a backdrop. Let the reader bring their own knowledge to the story, while you focus on personal narratives within the larger historical framework.

Crafting Characters That Ring True

Importantly, characters should belong to their era, influenced by the norms and values of the time. But flash fiction limits character development. How do you create believable, accurate characters in a few words?

Strategies:

1. Use Stereotypes, Then Subvert Them:

Start with a stereotype, like a dutiful Victorian wife or the 1920s flapper. Then, twist it—maybe the Victorian wife secretly writes suffragette pamphlets. This quickly establishes the character, and the twist adds depth.

2. Show Character Through Action:

With little backstory, let actions reveal your character. A woman defying societal norms by attending a forbidden rally speaks volumes about her personality and the pressures she faces.

3. Dialogue as a Character Window:

Let dialogue do double duty—revealing character and setting the historical scene. The way a character speaks, or their hesitation, can hint at their place in society and the era's constraints.

Plotting in a Pinch

The plot should draw on real events or cultural practices. The goal is to create a gripping, believable plot. How does one construct a self-contained story that remains true to its historical origins?

Strategies:

1. Focus on a Crisis or Turning Point:

Flash fiction excels when it seizes a moment of transformation. This could be a letter arriving with devastating news, a secret revealed, or a life-altering decision. These moments can tie into historical events but should be small enough to explore fully within the flash format.

2. Use Historical Figures Sparingly:

While tempting, well-known figures can dominate your story. If you include them, keep their role brief, letting your fictional characters shine. For example, a chance encounter with Abraham Lincoln at a train station could pivot your character's life without making Lincoln the star.

3. End with a Historical Echo:

Also end with a hint at what's coming. A character's decision should foreshadow a historical event, so the reader is left with a sense of connection to the broader narrative.

Okay so now we are ready to start writing, or are we? But before we dive in let's look at how to be original in Flash Fiction.

500 WORDS: WRITING ORIGINAL HISTORICAL FLASH FICTION

BRING NEW IDEAS TO YOUR WRITING

LET'S FACE IT—HISTORY IS a vast playground, yet writers often return to the same stories. Familiarity is comforting, sure, but why not venture into less-trodden paths? If you're looking to shake things up, here's a list of overdone historical topics, plus some fresh alternatives to inspire your next piece.

Overdone Historical Topics & Fresh Alternatives:

1. World War II – The Holocaust
Alternative: Explore World War II's impact on lesser-covered regions like South America or Southeast Asia. Delve into how the war affected indigenous communities, refugees, or local politics.

2. The Tudor Dynasty – Henry VIII and His Wives
Alternative: Focus on Empress Matilda's reign (1102–1167), who fought a civil war (The Anarchy) for the English throne, paving the way for future queens like Elizabeth I.

3. The American Civil War – Battles and Famous Generals
Alternative: Uncover the role of spies, particularly lesser-known female or African American spies, who played crucial roles in gathering intelligence.

4. Ancient Rome – The Fall of the Roman Empire

Alternative: Shift to the Byzantine Empire during Justinian I's reign. Explore the N. riots, the Hagia Sophia's construction, or Empress Theodora's influence on policy.

5. Victorian England – Jack the Ripper

Alternative: Investigate the Industrial Revolution's impact on rural England, where mechanization transformed small towns and farming communities, sparking resistance.

6. The French Revolution – The Reign of Terror

Alternative: Highlight the Haitian Revolution (1791–1804), where enslaved Africans successfully revolted against French rule, leading to the first independent black republic.

7. Medieval Europe – The Crusades

Alternative: Explore the rise and fall of the Almoravid Dynasty in North Africa and Spain, focusing on cultural and military clashes between Islamic sects and Christian kingdoms.

8. The American Wild West – Outlaws and Gunfights

Alternative: Tell the story of the California Gold Rush from the perspective of Chinese immigrants, examining their contributions and the discrimination they faced.

9. The Renaissance – The Life of Leonardo da Vinci

Alternative: Shine a light on women of the Renaissance—female artists, scientists, and thinkers who contributed to the era but were overshadowed by men.

10. The Russian Revolution – The Fall of the Romanovs

Alternative: Explore the lives of ordinary Russians during the subsequent Civil War (1917–1923) or the Kronstadt Rebellion of 1921, focusing on how these events affected peasants, workers, and soldiers.

Why Alternatives?

Overdone topics focus on well-known events or figures romanticized in popular culture. While compelling, they risk becoming repetitive unless approached from a unique angle.

These alternatives offer fresh perspectives by highlighting less-explored events, regions, or groups. They allow writers to tell new stories, bring underrepresented voices to the forefront, and breathe life into overlooked parts of history. By delving into these lesser-known areas, you can create historical fiction that's both original and enlightening, expanding the genre and introducing readers to fascinating aspects of history they might not know.

EXERCISES FOR HISTORICAL FLASH FICTION

HERE ARE SOME EXERCISES for you to practise your flash fiction.

1. Time Capsule Challenge

Goal: Nail that vivid imagery and atmosphere.

Exercise: Pick a historical period—think Victorian London, Ancient Egypt, or Renaissance Italy. Now, zoom in on one object from that time—a piece of jewellery, a tool, a letter.

Write a snappy 300-word flash fiction piece that brings this object to life. Don't over-explain—let the sights, sounds, and smells of the era do the talking. Make your readers feel like they're right there, holding that artifact.

2. Behind the Curtain

Goal: Get deep with character and subtext.

Exercise: Take a famous historical figure—Joan of Arc, Cleopatra, Galileo—but tell the story from the perspective of someone in their shadow. Maybe it's a servant, a friend, or even an enemy.

In 500 words, show us how this person sees the legend and how their life is shaped by them. Reveal the character's depth through what's left unsaid—let subtext do the heavy lifting.

3. History Remix GETTYSBUR &
STONEWALL

Goal: Flip the script on history.

Exercise: Pick a big historical event and give it a twist. What if a major battle went the other way? What if a famous figure made a different choice?

In 400 words, craft a flash fiction story that dives into this alternate history. Play with what readers think they know—surprise them, challenge them, and show them a new angle on the past.

MORE EXERCISES FOR HISTORICAL FLASH FICTION

TRY ONE OF THESE PLOTS.

HERE ARE FIVE PLOTS for original historical flash fiction for you to try and write.

1. A young Viking warrior returns home after a raid, only to find a Roman centurion's ghost guarding a treasure buried beneath his village.

2. During the Salem witch trials, a suspected witch secretly casts a spell to swap places with her accuser just before the verdict is read.

3. In ancient Egypt, a tomb painter discovers the pharaoh's final resting place will include a depiction of a betrayal he hasn't committed—yet.

4. On the eve of the French Revolution, a noblewoman discovers a peasant revolt plot hidden in the pattern of her new silk dress.

5. A Civil War soldier, on the brink of death, writes a letter that somehow arrives 150 years later, changing the life of a modern-day historian.

TIME TRAVEL – A WHOLE WORLD OF ITS OWN

A SUB-GENRE WHICH IS VERY APPEALING

TIME TRAVEL AND TIME shifts are staples of historical flash fiction. But how do you do them well? Time travel is where characters hop between different eras—past, present, or future—opening up a world of narrative possibilities.

Why Time Travel Works?

Time travel is like playing with history. It lets you:
- See how things were different and how they shape the present.
- Imagine "what if" scenarios—what if history went another way?
- Send characters back in time by accident or design or let them glimpse the future.
- Switch between past and present, showing their connections.

It's a creative playground where you can twist history in fun and unexpected ways.

Common Time Travel Tropes

When writing time travel, recognize that these stories have been told many times. That's not a bad thing—it just means you need to add a fresh twist or setting to make it stand out. Here are five popular time travel tropes and how to elevate them:

1. The "Butterfly Effect."

Description: A small change in the past leads to significant, often unforeseen, consequences in the future.

    Example: A traveller steps on a flower in ancient times, returning to a present where history has dramatically altered—governments have toppled, and technology has evolved in bizarre ways.

    Elevate It: What if the change creates a utopia instead of chaos?

2. The "Time Loop."

Description: A character is trapped in a repeating cycle, reliving the same day or moment over and over.

    Example: A scientist relives the day before a catastrophic event, desperately trying to stop it before the loop resets.

    Elevate It: Reveal a personal tragedy in each loop that the character didn't see coming.

3. The "Historical Intervention."

Description: A character travels back to alter a significant historical event, often grappling with the ethics of changing the past.

    Example: A historian tries to prevent an assassination that sparked a world war, only to face unintended consequences.

    Elevate It: What if their intervention is the very cause of the event they wanted to prevent?

4. The "Future Shock"

Description: A character travels to the future and is overwhelmed by how much the world has changed.

    Example: A person from the 1800s finds themselves in the 22nd century, navigating advanced technology and alien species.

Elevate It: What if the future isn't as advanced as it seems, and the character holds the key to fixing it?

5. The "Grandfather Paradox"

Description: A time traveller's actions in the past threaten their own existence, creating a paradox.

Example: A man goes back to stop his grandfather's tragic death, risking his own future.

Elevate It: Create a self-consistent universe where the traveller's actions were always part of history or embrace the paradox to explore deep moral dilemmas.

The "grandfather paradox" is a common plot device in time travel and temporal displacement short fiction. The paradox states that if a time traveller were to go back in time and kill their own grandfather before their parent was conceived, then they would not exist and therefore would not be able to go back in time to commit the act. This creates a paradox in which the very act of traveling back in time could prevent the time traveller from ever existing.

This paradox has been explored in many time travel and time shift stories, and it presents a unique challenge for writers. On one hand, the paradox provides an interesting and thought-provoking plot device that can drive the narrative forward. On the other hand, it can be difficult to write a story that uses the paradox without falling into the trap of contradictions and inconsistencies.

One way that writers can navigate the grandfather paradox is by creating a self-consistent time travel or time shift universe. This means that the events of the past are predetermined and cannot be changed, and any actions taken by the time traveller were always part of history. This approach can provide a satisfying resolution to the paradox while still allowing for interesting and unexpected twists in the plot.

Another approach is to embrace the paradox and use it as a central theme in the story. The time traveller may become obsessed with the idea of changing history and preventing their own existence, leading to a moral dilemma and a complex exploration of the consequences of time travel.

Ultimately, the grandfather paradox in time travel and time shift short fiction can provide a rich and engaging theme for writers to explore. By carefully considering the implications of time travel and creating a self-consistent universe or embracing the paradox, writers can create compelling stories that push the boundaries of the genre.

Exercises for Time Travel Flash Fiction

Try some of these plots

Here are some ideas for Time Travel flash fiction that you might want to try.

1. A boy in the 1950s finds a comic book predicting his life, including his future wife and career.

2. A modern-day archaeologist finds a mysterious device that sends him back to ancient Egypt, where he meets the pharaoh and learns a shocking secret.

3. A soldier in World War II is wounded and wakes up in a hospital in 2023, where he meets his grandson, who is also a soldier.

4. A medieval knight finds a portal that leads him to a futuristic city, where he is mistaken for a superhero.

5. A girl in the present day receives a letter from her grandmother who died 10 years ago, telling her to follow a series of clues that will reveal a family secret.

100 WORDS: AN INTRODUCTION TO FANTASY FLASH FICTION

LET'S GET STARTED

WRITING FANTASY FLASH FICTION is a thrilling challenge.

It's all about crafting new worlds, magical systems, and characters with just a few strokes. The trick? Build a believable, immersive world fast. You've got to nail pacing and plot in the tightest space. Every word counts—exposition, action, dialogue—all working double time.

The real magic? Balancing rich world-building with sharp, punchy storytelling. Dive into themes, question morality, or offer pure escapism.

In this condensed form, fantasy becomes a playground for bold ideas and impactful narratives.

In Fantasy, the possibilities are infinite, and the reward? A wild escape for every imagination.

850 Words: Writing Fantasy Flash Fiction

The Art of World-Building in a Few Words

Creating a Vivid Setting Quickly

WORLD-BUILDING IS THE BACKBONE of fantasy, but in flash fiction, every word has to earn its place. Your job? Paint a whole world in a handful of sentences. Focus on sensory details that pack a punch—think "blue-tinged fog clinging to obsidian spires." One image, a whole vibe. Or take a familiar element, give it a twist: "silver-leafed trees whispering ancient songs." You're not just describing; you're igniting imaginations. But don't let the world steal the show. Blend those details with action or dialogue—"merchants hawking enchanted wares under starlight lanterns"—and keep your story front and center.

Example: "The air shimmered with golden dust, as twin moons cast their glow over the towering crystal cliffs. Beneath them, a river of liquid light whispered ancient secrets."

Balancing World-Building with Story

In flash fiction, world-building must work double-time. It's tempting to create a sprawling epic, but you've got maybe 1,000 words—tops. Go for "world-building in the margins." Drop hints like "the Crimson War" or a "dragon-forged blade." These subtle cues make your world feel bigger than the words on the page. Keep everything tied to your plot. If your character faces a moral dilemma, let the world's rigid laws intensify their struggle. Precision is key. A few well-chosen details can make your world rich and immersive, without drowning your narrative.

Example: "As she unsheathed her sword, its edge crackling with the power of fallen stars, she remembered the tales of the Lost Kingdom. The legends were true, but now wasn't the time to dwell on history."

Conveying Complex Characters Efficiently

In flash fiction, character development needs to be lean and mean. Introduce characters through actions that reveal who they are, fast. A protagonist healing a wounded animal with a spell? You've nailed compassion and magical prowess in one move. Dialogue's your other weapon—"I've crossed the Shadowlands for less" tells us volumes in just a few words. Flash fiction is all about those pivotal moments—show a character's inner turmoil, like betraying their kind for redemption, and you've delivered complexity without filler.

Example: "With a flick of her wrist, the sorceress healed the bird's broken wing, but the tears in her eyes hinted at a deeper, hidden wound. Her magic could mend others, but never herself."

Archetypes and Tropes

Archetypes are your best friends in flash fiction—they give readers an instant sense of who's who. But don't let them go stale. Your grizzled warrior could secretly love gardening. Flip the script. A chosen one who resists their destiny? Now you're adding depth. Use tropes as your foundation, but build on them with fresh, specific details. That way, you keep your characters both recognizable and intriguingly unique.

Example: "The dark knight was clad in black stained armor, but concealed within his breastplate were secret letters revealed a forbidden love for the enemy princess. Duty called him to this battle, for he knew sometimes only force of arms brought peace. "Spare the small folk," he called as he led the charge."

Keeping the Plot Simple Yet Impactful

In flash fiction, plots need to be razor-sharp. Focus on a single, powerful conflict or event. A character using forbidden magic to save someone? Boom—instant stakes, instant tension. Stick to plots that unfold in real-time. Flash fiction shines in capturing pivotal moments—when the heat is on, and every decision counts.

Example: "The moment she whispered the forbidden incantation, the world shifted, and the stars aligned to grant her wish—at a terrible cost. She had saved him, but at the price of her own soul."

Implying a Larger World or Conflict

Even with a simple plot, hint at a bigger world. Mention "wars in northern kingdoms" or a "Mount Xyron-forged blade" to suggest a grander scale. Leave some threads hanging, inviting readers to imagine the next chapter. Your plot might be small, but it should feel like a doorway to something bigger.

Example: "The distant rumble of drums signaled the approach of the Shadow Army, yet the village remained unaware. This battle was just one skirmish in a war that spanned the continents."

Using Language to Enhance the Fantasy

Language in fantasy flash fiction should do double duty—setting the scene and evoking magic. Use metaphors and sensory details to transport your reader: "trees whispering secrets, leaves glowing like embers." But don't get bogged down. Every word should spark imagination without slowing the pace.

Example: "The forest was alive with the scent of damp earth and blooming night-shade, each breath a spell that pulled her deeper into its embrace. The trees weren't just trees—they were ancient guardians."

Tone and Atmosphere

Tone sets the stage. Whether it's dark and ominous or light and whimsical, your language and imagery need to align. A crumbling castle or a lively market? It all shapes the mood. Keep the tone consistent, from the first sentence to the last, and your world will pulse with life.

Example: "The sun dipped below the horizon, leaving the world bathed in a blood-red glow. The darkness that followed wasn't just the absence of light, but the presence of something far more sinister."

500 words: Know your Genres in Fantasy Flash Fiction

Something you know but need to Master

Fantasy is a genre of fiction that deals with imaginary worlds, supernatural events, and magical creatures. It can range from epic high fantasy, with sprawling worlds and intricate mythologies, to dystopian fantasy, with dark, oppressive societies and broken characters. Writing fantasy flash fiction can be a delightful challenge for authors, as it requires creating vivid, fantastical worlds and intriguing characters in a condensed form.

Common Subgenres of Fantasy

Do you know your genre? Fantasy may be the realm of magic and unicorns, dragons and dwarfs, but it has its rules, and fans of the fantasy genre are very keen to read fiction that meets their expectations. So, in the first instance, can you define your fantasy genre?

Here are the five biggies:

Epic fantasy

Often features sprawling worlds, complex political systems, and intricate magic systems. Epic fantasy stories can span multiple volumes and can take years to complete. Examples of epic fantasy include J.R.R. Tolkien's "The Lord of the Rings" and George R.R. Martin's "A Song of Ice and Fire" series. Writing epic fantasy flash fiction requires the author to condense the world-building and character development that usually takes place over multiple volumes into a single, impactful story. This can be a challenge, but it also allows authors to experiment with new storytelling techniques and focus on the core elements of their epic fantasy world.

Examples:

- The Way of Kings" by Brandon Sanderson

- "Throne of Glass" by Sarah J. Maas (2012)

Dystopian fantasy

Deals with oppressive societies, broken characters, and a lack of hope. Examples of dystopian fantasy include Suzanne Collins' "The Hunger Games" and Margaret Atwood's "The Handmaid's Tale." Writing dystopian fantasy flash fiction allows authors to explore the darker sides of humanity and society in a condensed form. The challenge in writing dystopian fantasy flash fiction is creating a believable world and compelling characters while still conveying the story's themes and messages.

Examples:

- The Hunger Games by Suzanne Collins

- The Dark Tower: The Gunslinger by Stephen King

Urban fantasy

Typically takes place in a contemporary urban setting and features supernatural elements such as vampires, werewolves, and magic. The stories often involve the interaction between the supernatural and the human world and explore themes of identity, morality, and power.

Examples:

- Rivers of London" by Ben Aaronovitch 500 words

- Harry Potter and the Order of the Pheonix" by JK Rowling

Magical realism

Where magical or supernatural elements are incorporated into a realistic setting. In this type of fantasy fiction, the magic is often subtle and understated, and presented as a normal part of everyday life rather than something extraordinary. The magical elements may not be explained or rationalized and are often used to explore deeper themes and emotions. This genre blurs the lines between reality and fantasy, creating a dreamlike atmosphere that challenges the reader's perceptions of what is possible.

Examples:

- "The Lion, the Witch and the Wardrobe" by C.S. Lewis

- "The Fellowship of the Ring" by J.R.R. Tolkien

500 words: Know your Tropes in Fantasy

Tropes are the story arcs so familiar to Fantasy readers

ABOVE WE SPOKE ABOUT sub-genres within Fantasy it is also important to know the common tropes in Fantasy, i.e. the story arcs and characters that make an appearance again and again.

It is important to know and understand tropes or story lines because two reasons:

- Your reader will recognise a story arc, and be reading in expectation of an expected conclusion

- You as the writer have to think about your reader, and decide whether you will meet their expectations, and stick to a well-loved story line, or whether to subvert that story line but bring the reader onto another story line that has another unexpected conclusion.

Not thinking of story arcs and how your readers perceive, read and enjoy them, will lead you to writing fiction that can be perfect in many well, but is strangely unsatisfying.

Story Telling, story arcs, tropes are key to making a story work.

So here we go, here are the most frequently encountered tropes in fantasy short fiction:

The "Reluctant Hero."

Description: An ordinary character who is thrust into an extraordinary situation, often against their will, and must rise to the occasion to save their world or others. This trope explores themes of courage, growth, and destiny.

Example: A humble blacksmith's apprentice discovers they are the last of an ancient bloodline capable of wielding a powerful magic and must fight to protect their village from an impending dark force.

The "Magical Mentor"

Description: A wise, often mysterious figure who guides the protagonist on their journey, teaching them about the magical world and helping them unlock their potential. This mentor usually has a deep connection to the world's lore and might carry their own secrets.

Example: An elderly sorcerer who lives on the edge of the enchanted forest takes a young, unsuspecting traveller under their wing, teaching them the ways of magic as they prepare for a looming conflict.

The "Hidden World"

Description: A secret, magical world exists alongside the ordinary one, accessible only to those who know where to look. This trope often involves a character discovering this hidden world and becoming embroiled in its conflicts and wonders.

Example: A young librarian finds a hidden door in the back of the library that leads to a parallel world where mythical creatures and ancient magic still thrive, but the balance of power is dangerously shifting.

The "Quest for a Lost Artifact"

Description: The characters embark on a dangerous journey to find a powerful, often ancient, object that can alter the fate of their world. This trope often involves trials, riddles, and battles, with the artifact serving as both a prize and a burden.

Example: A band of misfit adventurers must track down an ancient, enchanted sword that is said to be the only weapon capable of defeating the dark lord threatening their realm.

The "Prophecy Fulfilled"

Description: The story revolves around an ancient prophecy that foretells the coming of a hero, the rise of a dark power, or a great change in the world. The characters must navigate their roles within this prophecy, whether to fulfil or subvert it.

Example: A farmhand learns they are the prophesied "Chosen One" destined to defeat a resurrected dragon, but the prophecy's true meaning unravels as they face moral dilemmas and unexpected allies.

Remember fantasy tropes and story arcs are beloved because they tap into the sense of wonder, adventure, and the battle between good and evil that defines the genre, while also allowing room for rich world-building and character development in a short format.

Exercises for Fantasy Flash Fiction

Time to get writing

Here are some exercises to practice your Fantasy Flash Fiction.

Magic in the Mundane:

Write a 500-word story where a fantastical element is hidden within an ordinary setting. Think about a regular coffee shop where one of the baristas can read minds, or a laundromat where the washing machines transport clothes to another dimension. The goal is to blend the magical with the every day seamlessly.

World-Building in a Paragraph:

Create a rich, vivid fantasy world in just one paragraph. Focus on a specific location—like a market, a forest, or a castle. Use sensory details to evoke the atmosphere, and hint at the culture, history, or magic of the place without explaining everything outright.

A Hero's Dilemma:

Write a flash story (300-500 words) where a classic fantasy hero faces a moral dilemma. They could be a knight deciding whether to slay a dragon or a wizard choosing between power and love. Keep the focus on their internal struggle and resolve it within the constraints of the story.

Fantasy Magical Castle exercise.

Below are the descriptions of three magical castles: Hogwarts School, Rivendell and Disneyland. Can you determine which one is which? What are the small details that give you a clue to its identity, and differentiates one from another?

1. <Missing word> loomed in the distance, its turrets piercing the dusky sky, as if reaching for the stars. The scent of damp earth and ancient parchment filled the air, mingling with the faint whiff of something sweet and magical—perhaps a charm gone slightly awry. The stone walls, weathered and wise, hummed with secrets, whispering tales of mischief and bravery. Golden lights twinkled in the windows, hinting at bustling corridors and cozy common rooms. The banners of the four houses fluttered in the cool breeze, each crest telling stories as old as the castle itself. The road cleaner paused, broom in hand, gazing up at Hogwarts, where the ordinary met the extraordinary.

2. The castle stood tall and proud, its gleaming turrets piercing the evening sky, as though crafted by Elven hands in ages long past. The air was heavy with the fragrance of roses, mingling with the sweet aroma of confections, while the stones whispered of olden days, their voices like the distant murmur of ancient lore. Within the high-arched windows, warm lights flickered, casting shadows that danced to tunes forgotten by the world of men. Weathered banners, adorned with symbols of once-great realms, fluttered in the cool evening breeze. Beneath it all, the ground was paved not with mere stone, but with the echoes of a thousand joyous footsteps. With a weary sigh, the road cleaner, his task humble yet enduring, swept the path before the gates of <missing word>, where even memories of forgotten ages linger.

3. The castle loomed against the twilight sky, its spires spiralling upward like enchanted needles stitching stars into the heavens. The air shimmered with the scent of roses and spun sugar, while whispers of ancient spells clung to the stone walls, their words lost to time. Windows flickered with the soft glow of lanterns, where ghostly figures waltzed to melodies unheard by mortal ears. Banners,

worn and tattered, fluttered in the breeze, each bearing symbols of kingdoms long forgotten. The ground beneath was not cobblestone but paved in dreams, where every step echoed a child's laugh. The road cleaner sighed, pushing his broom past the gates of <missing word>.

More Exercises for Fantasy Flash Fiction

Story plots for you to try your hand at.

Here are a number of plots groups by genre of fantasy fiction.

Epic Fantasy

- **The Quest:** A hero sets out on a dangerous mission to retrieve a magical artifact that is the key to saving their kingdom from destruction.

- **The Chosen One:** A young person discovers that they are the only one who can defeat an ancient evil that threatens their world, but they must first learn to control their newfound powers.

- **The Rebellion:** A group of rebels band together to overthrow an oppressive regime that has taken over their land, using their unique abilities to launch a daring attack against their oppressors.

- **The Curse:** A character is cursed by a powerful sorcerer or witch and must find a way to break the curse before it destroys their life and everything, they hold dear.

- **The Portal:** A character discovers a mysterious portal that transports them to another world or dimension, where they must navigate strange new lands and battle unknown dangers to find their way back home.

Dystopian Fantasy

- **In a world where magic is forbidden,** a group of rebel's band together to reclaim their magical heritage and overthrow the oppressive government.

- **After a virus wipes out most of humanity,** the remaining survivors must navigate a harsh and dangerous landscape to find a rumoured sanctuary, but soon discover that the sanctuary is not what it seems.

- **In a society where people are genetically modified to be perfect,** a teenage girl struggles to fit in because of her imperfections. When she discovers a secret rebellion fighting against the genetic modifications, she must decide whether to join them and risk everything she knows or continue living as an outcast.

Magical Realism Fantasy

- **A woman discovers that she can communicate with animals** but struggles to convince others of her ability until a group of animals help her solve a mystery.

- **A man wakes up one morning to find that his body has been transformed into that of a tree.** As he adjusts to his new form, he begins to experience a deeper connection with nature.

- **A young girl discovers that she has the power to bring inanimate objects to life.** As she explores her ability, she begins to realize the consequences of her actions and the responsibility that comes with her power.

Urban Fantasy

- **A young woman discovers she has the power to see and communicate with ghosts.** When she moves into a new apartment in a haunted building, she must navigate the complex web of relationships between the living and the dead while trying to unravel the mystery of why the building is haunted in the first place.

- **In a world where humans and supernatural creatures live side by side, a** human detective is assigned to a case involving the murder of a werewolf. As she investigates the crime, she must confront her own prejudices and assumptions about the supernatural while working with a werewolf partner who challenges her every step of the way.

- **A group of friends stumble upon a hidden portal to a magical realm in the heart of the city. As** they explore this mysterious new world, they discover that the magic that sustains it is slowly fading away. With the help of a wise old wizard, they must find a way to restore the magic before it's too late.

- **After a mysterious illness wipes out most of the population,** a small community of survivors in a city apartment building discovers that they have all developed strange and powerful abilities. As they learn to control their powers and work together to survive, they must also contend with the dangerous gangs and cults that have taken over the city.

Gettysburg
Ghosts

100 Words: An Introduction to Romance in Flash Fiction

And They All Lived Happily Ever After?

WELCOME TO THE WHIRLWIND world of romance in flash fiction—where love stories unfold in just a heartbeat.

In this chapter, we'll explore how to capture the intensity, passion, and heartbreak of romance in a few powerful words. Whether it's the spark of first love, the tension of unspoken desires, or the bittersweet farewell, romance in flash fiction is all about distilling the essence of relationships into short, unforgettable moments.

Get ready to dive into the art of crafting love stories that linger long after the final word, proving that sometimes, less is truly more.

> In romance flash fiction, love ignites in a single sentence and burns bright forever.

820 WORDS: WRITING ROMANCE FLASH FICTION

THE DELICATE DANCE OF LOVE, SEX AND DEATH

Building Emotional Punch with Fewer Words

IN ROMANCE FLASH FICTION, it's all about packing that emotional punch. With no space for long-winded backstories, zoom in on a single, powerful moment—whether it's the first meeting, a sudden realization, or that final goodbye.

To crank up the emotional intensity, lean on subtext and suggestion. Skip the melodrama—show a character hesitating over a text that simply says, "I'm happy for you." Those three words can speak volumes about unrequited love or the heartache of letting go.

Keep your dialogue tight and loaded with meaning. One line can sum up an entire relationship. A simple "Do you remember?" can stir up shared memories, lost time, and nostalgia—all in just three words.

An Example:

She started to type her reply. Then deleted it hurriedly. She started again jabbing at the phone. Delete. She took a breath, and typed "I'm happy for you,". Switching off her phone she slips it into her handbag, she'll find it later, for now she has to find a handkerchief to blot and wipe the tears running down her face.

Character Snapshots: Glimpses and Gestures

Flash fiction doesn't do long character arcs, but that doesn't mean your characters can't jump off the page. In romance, character depth often comes from the little things—a lingering glance, a near-accidental touch, or a nervous habit.

Imagine a character's hand trembling as they reach for their partner's. Vulnerability, longing, fear—it's all there in that one gesture. These moments let readers connect emotionally without needing a whole novel's worth of backstory.

Play with contrasts to highlight traits. A normally composed character who fumbles around their crush? That shows some deep feelings right there. And don't be afraid to tweak familiar archetypes—a stoic protector who's afraid of the dark or a free-spirited artist with a practical side. These twists add layers without taking up space.

An Example:

As he reached for her hand, the usually steady cup slipped from his grasp, coffee splashing between them. Their fingers brushed in the chaos, just long enough for her to feel the tremor that betrayed his nerves.

Plotting Romance in a Flash

In flash fiction, your plot needs to be sharp and impactful, zeroing in on a key moment in the relationship. Whether it's the joy of a first kiss, the tension of a lingering conflict, or the bittersweet farewell, focus on capturing that moment's essence.

The plot often hinges on a turning point—a confession, a realization, or a decision. Maybe two characters finally admit their feelings, or one decides to let go for the other's happiness. These moments pack emotional weight, perfect for a quick, deep dive.

Don't spell everything out—let readers fill in the blanks. Hint at a shared history through dialogue or interactions, allowing their imagination to do some heavy lifting. This not only adds depth but also draws the reader deeper into the story.

An example:

She placed the key on the table, the silence between them louder than any words. As the door clicked shut behind her, its final echo filled the empty space he would now call home.

Setting the Mood with Words

Language is your secret weapon in romance flash fiction. The right word or phrase can set the whole mood. Whether you're aiming for tender and warm or intense and passionate, your word choices should hit the right emotional notes.

For a sweet, heartwarming vibe, go for soft, lyrical language—like describing a sunset as "a blush spreading across the sky" or a touch as "feather-light." For something more intense, turn up the heat with bolder words— "her pulse raced like a storm" or "his kiss burned away all doubt."

The setting matters too. A secluded beach, a cozy café, or a bustling street each brings its own romantic tone. You don't need paragraphs of description—just pick the right backdrop to instantly set the scene and support the story's emotion.

An example:
Under the café's awning, they finally met, rain-soaked streets shimmering in the soft glow of streetlights. The world around them faded, leaving only the warmth of their reunion in the cool night air.

The Beauty of Brevity in Romance

Romance in flash fiction shows the true power of brevity. With just a handful of words, you can stir deep emotions, sketch out complex characters, and craft plots that linger in the reader's mind long after the last word.

Writing romance in this tight format pushes you to focus on the essentials—emotion, connection, and those pivotal moments that define relationships. As you dive into romance flash fiction, remember: less is more. Trust your readers to catch the subtleties and aim to capture the heart of a relationship in one, powerful moment—a moment as timeless as love itself.

An example:
The morning light caught the words scrawled on the pillow's edge—"I'll be back." She stared at the letter, her heart wavering between hope and doubt, wondering if the promise would ever be fulfilled.

325 WORDS: CLICHES IN ROMANCE FLASH FICTION

MASTER CLICHES TO ENHANCE YOUR WRITING

CLICHÉS IN ROMANCE FLASH fiction are a double-edged sword—they can offer comfort and familiarity, but they can also lead to predictable, stale storytelling. Leaning too heavily on clichés might box your characters into stereotypes and drain the life out of your narrative. But here's the thing: when used with a twist, a well-placed cliché can be a shortcut to instant connection with your readers, providing a quick emotional hook. The trick is to take that familiar trope and flip it on its head—give it a fresh spin, surprise your audience, and keep your story original and engaging.

So, let's start by knowing what a cliché is – here is a list:

1. The love triangle

2. The bad boy with a heart of gold

3. The insta-love or love at first sight connection

4. The billionaire or prince charming rescuing the damsel in distress

5. The love-hate relationship or opposites attract dynamic

6. The best friend-turned-lover

7. The big misunderstanding or ex-lover drama

8. The makeover transformation or secret baby reveal

9. The "meet cute" scenario with cliched romantic gestures

10. The happily ever after or "love conquers all" ending

Here's how to avoid writing cliches:

Identify the cliche:

The first step is to recognize the cliche you want to work with. This could be anything from the love triangle to the friends-to-lovers trope.

Look for unique angles:

Once you have identified the cliche, start brainstorming ways to put a unique spin on it. Think about how you can subvert expectations or take the story in a different direction than what is expected.

Focus on character development:

No matter what cliche you are working with; strong character development is key to making your story stand out. Consider what makes your characters unique and what drives their actions and motivations.

Take risks:

Finally, don't be afraid to take risks and push the boundaries of the cliche you are working with. Sometimes the most memorable stories come from taking bold creative risks and trying something new.

325 WORDS: KNOW YOUR TROPES IN ROMANCE FLASH FICTION

STORYTELLING, STORY ARCS AND TROPES YOU SHOULD KNOW

HERE ARE THE TOP five tropes or story arcs commonly found in romance short fiction

1. The "Opposites Attract."

Description: Two characters with contrasting personalities or lifestyles who are drawn to each other despite (or because of) their differences. The tension between them often leads to conflict, but also sparks a deeper connection.

   Example: A free-spirited artist falls for a disciplined, by-the-book lawyer, and their differences challenge both of them to grow.

2. The "Second Chance at Love."

Description: Characters who were once in love but parted ways due to circumstances, misunderstandings, or personal issues, are reunited and given another opportunity to rekindle their romance.

Example: High school sweethearts meet again years later at a reunion, realizing they still have feelings for each other despite the time and distance.

3. The "Friends to Lovers."

Description: A deep, platonic friendship evolves into a romantic relationship as the characters realize their feelings for each other have changed, often gradually and unexpectedly.

Example: Two best friends who've been inseparable since childhood start to see each other in a new light after one of them begins dating someone else.

4. The "Fake Relationship."

Description: Two characters agree to pretend they are in a romantic relationship for various reasons—social pressure, to avoid awkward situations, or to make someone else jealous—only to end up falling for each other for real.

Example: A woman asks her colleague to pose as her boyfriend at a family wedding, but the line between pretence and reality quickly blurs.

5. The "Love Triangle."

Description: A romantic situation where one character is torn between two potential love interests, creating tension, drama, and difficult choices. This trope explores themes of desire, loyalty, and self-discovery.

Example: A woman finds herself caught between her reliable, long-term boyfriend and an exciting, mysterious new suitor.

These romance tropes are popular because they tap into the emotional complexities of love and relationships, providing fertile ground for conflict, growth, and ultimately, satisfying resolutions.

DEEP DIVE: THE ART OF DIALOGUE IN ROMANCE FLASH FICTION

WHERE A SILENCE SAYS AS MUCH AS THE WORDS

Deep Dive: The Art of Dialogue in Romance Flash Fiction

DIALOGUE IN ROMANCE FLASH fiction isn't just about what's being said—it's about what's not being said. In the tight confines of flash fiction, every word counts, and the spaces between the words are just as important. Great romantic dialogue is like an iceberg: the real weight is hidden beneath the surface, layered with unspoken love, simmering lust, or seething anger. Let's dive into how to make your dialogue crackle with emotion, tension, and meaning.

Example 1: The Unspoken Confession

Scenario: Two old friends meet after years apart. Both have feelings they've never expressed.

Dialogue:

"It's been a while, hasn't it?" she says, her eyes tracing the edge of his coffee cup instead of his face.

"Yeah," he replies, the word heavy with everything he's never said. *"You look good, happy."*

She smiles, but it doesn't reach her eyes. *"Happy enough. And you? Still chasing those dreams?"*

He shrugs, his fingers tightening around the cup. *"Not all of them."*

"Some dreams aren't meant to be caught," she whispers, finally meeting his gaze.

"No," he says, leaning in just a fraction too close. *"Some are meant to haunt you forever."*

Analysis: Here, the dialogue dances around a confession neither is brave enough to make. The tension simmers in what's left unsaid—their shared past, the love they never admitted, and the ache that lingers between them. The words are simple, but the emotions they carry are heavy, leaving the reader to feel the weight of their unresolved feelings.

Example 2: The Bitter Goodbye

Scenario: A couple on the brink of separation, struggling between anger and love.

Dialogue:

"So, this is it?" she says, her voice barely above a whisper, the packed suitcase between them like a wall.

"I guess it is," he replies, trying to keep the bitterness from his voice and failing. *"You're really leaving?"*

"I don't see another choice," she snaps, but her eyes are glassy, betraying the anger in her voice. *"Do you?"*

He swallows hard, looking at her as if seeing her for the last time. *"No. I guess we've made our choices."*

"You did," she fires back, her hand resting on the suitcase handle, gripping it like a lifeline. *"You made yours when you chose work over us."*

His shoulders slump, defeated. *"And you chose to leave instead of fight."*

They stand in silence, the words they've spoken echoing in the space between them. Finally, she turns, her voice breaking. *"I hope you find what you're looking for."*

"I already did," he whispers to the empty room as she walks out the door.

Analysis: This dialogue crackles with the rawness of a relationship unravelling. Every word is loaded with anger, regret, and unspoken love. Their exchange is filled with accusations, but also with a lingering sense that things could have been different. The dialogue is sharp, but the real story lies in the emotions they're both struggling to hide.

Example 3: The Heated Argument

Scenario: Two lovers, caught in the heat of an argument, with desire simmering just beneath the surface.

Dialogue:

"You never listen to me!" she shouts, slamming the door behind her, her chest heaving.

"Maybe if you had something worth saying, I would!" he fires back, eyes blazing, but there's a flicker of something else there too.

"Is that what you think?" she hisses, stepping closer, her voice dropping to a dangerous whisper. *"That I'm just some noise in your life?"*

He steps forward too, close enough to feel the heat of her anger—and something more. *"No. I think you're the one thing I can't control, and it drives me crazy."*

She stops, stunned by his admission. *"So, what now?"* she asks, her voice softer but no less intense.

His hand reaches out, brushing her cheek, the anger melting into something else entirely. *"Now we see where this goes."*

Analysis: This dialogue is electric with anger and desire, both emotions battling for control. The argument is more than just words—it's a confrontation of deeper feelings that neither is willing to fully admit. The tension is palpable, but so is the attraction. The dialogue keeps the reader on edge, waiting to see if the anger will burn out or spark something more.

Wrapping Up

In romance flash fiction, dialogue is your secret weapon. It's not just about what your characters say—it's about what they can't say, won't say, or desperately want to say. Keep it sharp, keep it loaded, and let the unspoken emotions simmer beneath the surface. Whether it's love, lust, or anger, the right words—and the right silences—can turn a simple conversation into a moment that lingers long after the story ends.

Exercises for Romance Flash Fiction

Let's Get Writing

Here are some exercises to help you improve your Romance Flash Fiction.

First Meetings:

Write a 500-word story about two characters meeting for the first time. Focus on capturing the spark or connection in this brief encounter—whether it's love at first sight, a missed opportunity, or something more complex. Show their emotions through dialogue, body language, or small actions.

Love Letters:

Imagine one character writing a heartfelt letter to another, confessing something important—whether it's love, regret, or a secret. Keep it under 300 words and try to convey the depth of their feelings through the letter's tone, word choice, and what's left unsaid.

A Moment in Time:

Craft a short story (under 500 words) that encapsulates a single, significant moment in a romantic relationship. It could be a first kiss, a final goodbye, or the moment they realize they love each other. Focus on the emotions and sensory details, and let this moment stand as a complete story.

Examples of Cute-Meets.

Setting up the characters and setting in just a few words. The next three examples include a cute meet in 70s London, in Regency England, New York in 2021 and 17th century Japan.

Can you identify each one, and why does it work?

- Amid the swirl of patterned fabrics and psychedelic colours, she knocked over a rack of bellbottom jeans, sending them tumbling into the smiling shop assistant's arms. "Looks like fashion has a funny way of bringing people together," he quipped as their eyes met over the chaos.

- At the ball, Jane Bennet was dismayed to find herself spun into Mr. Darcy's arms, her forced smile barely concealing her discomfort. "It seems fate has paired us, Miss Bennet," he noted, while she silently wished the dance would end as quickly as it began.

- In the eerie quiet of the nearly empty New York subway during the 2021 shutdown, she fumbled with her mask and dropped her coffee, splashing it across his crisp white sneakers. Flustered, she mumbled an apology from a safe distance, but he just smiled and said, "Even in lockdown, it seems we're destined to start on the right foot.

- In a secluded grove outside Osaka, where cherry blossoms floated gently to the ground, she took refuge from the spring wind beneath a tree, only to discover a young samurai already standing there, his robe dusted with petals. As their eyes met, he offered her a place beside him, murmuring, "The blossoms, it seems, wished for us to meet in their fleeting moment of beauty."

More Exercises for Romance Flash Fiction

Try one of these Romance plots

Here are five plots for romance flash fiction, remember to make it your own:

1. **Second chance at love:** Two former lovers unexpectedly reunite after years apart and must confront their unresolved feelings and the reasons for their separation.

2. **Forbidden love:** A romance between two people from different worlds, whether it's due to social class, race, or even species, is tested by the disapproval of those around them.

3. **Love at first sight:** Two strangers meet and instantly fall in love but must navigate the challenges of building a relationship in a short amount of time.

4. **Long distance love:** A couple must navigate the difficulties of maintaining a relationship while living far apart from each other, whether it's due to work, school, or other circumstances.

5. **Friends to lovers:** Two friends who have known each other for years begin to realize their feelings for each other go beyond friendship, but fear that taking their relationship to the next level could ruin their friendship.

100 WORDS: AN INTRODUCTION TO WRITING SCIENCE FICTION FLASH FICTION

WRITING FROM A GALAXY FAR FAR AWAY.

SCIENCE FICTION AIMS TO capture and expand the imagination. From exploring new worlds to predicting future technologies, science fiction can provide a thought-provoking look into the future or a morality tale to reflect on the world we live in today.

Science Fiction flash fiction needs to create immersive, thought-provoking stories with just a handful of words. It's all about distilling complex concepts into sharp narratives that leave readers thinking long after the last line. In this chapter, we'll explore how to craft mini-universes, focus on tight world-building, with impressive characters, and plots that punch.

In science fiction, the stakes are sky-high—condense the infinite into a story that's unforgettable.

500 WORDS: WRITING SCIENCE FICTION FLASH FICTION

IN A DISTANT GALAXY...

Jumping into Sci-Fi Flash Fiction

SCIENCE FICTION IS YOUR ticket to explore wild, speculative worlds—but in flash fiction, you've got to do it in under 1,000 words. No pressure, right? The trick is to ditch the endless exposition and focus on the core of your story. In this chapter, we're diving into how to craft tight, impactful sci-fi flash fiction. We'll break down how to build worlds with a few sharp details, create relatable characters in strange settings, and plot with laser precision.

World-Building in a Flash

World-building is the heartbeat of sci-fi, but in flash fiction, you've got to do it fast. No room for sprawling descriptions—just drop in a few evocative details and let the reader's imagination do the heavy lifting. Mention "neon-lit skyscrapers piercing the smog" or "hover cars weaving through air traffic," and boom—your world is alive. Start in the middle of the action, and let the setting reveal itself naturally.

    Example: "Neon-lit skyscrapers pierced the smog-choked sky as he adjusted the bio-interface, the city humming beneath his feet."

Simplifying Complex Sci-Fi Concepts

Sci-fi loves big ideas—time travel, AI, genetic engineering. But in flash fiction, you need to simplify. Skip the tech manual; show the impact. Don't explain how the time machine works—show the paradox it creates or the ethical dilemma it triggers. Use metaphors or analogies to make complex concepts click instantly.

Example: "He downloaded memories like files into his new body, the process smooth—almost too smooth."

Relatable Characters in Alien Worlds

Your characters might be lightyears away from Earth, but their emotions should hit home. Focus on universal feelings—fear, love, loss. Even in a society of robots, a character grappling with their humanity is relatable. Dialogue and internal monologue are your best friends here. One line can reveal a world of emotion and motivation.

Example: "As the AI integrated with her mind, she whispered, 'Will I still be... me?'"

Precision Plotting

Sci-fi flash fiction demands a plot with laser focus. Pick one big idea and dive deep—no room for sprawling subplots. Whether it's a human-AI relationship or the ethics of cloning, your story should revolve around that central conflict. And don't forget the twist—a revelation that flips everything on its head.

Example: "In the end, he wasn't human at all—just the last experiment of a forgotten civilization."

Language that Sets the Mood

Your language should match the speculative vibe of your story. Use neologisms sparingly but effectively to evoke a futuristic world. The tone of your language can set the entire mood—clean and precise for a utopia, gritty and fragmented for a dystopia.

Example: "The quantum tether snapped, leaving the colony adrift in the void."

Mastering the Mini Universe

Writing sci-fi flash fiction is all about condensing the cosmos into a bite-sized story that still packs a punch. By focusing on tight world-building, simplified concepts, and a plot that zeroes in on one powerful idea, you can create stories that stick with your readers long after they've finished. Embrace the constraints, and you'll find that the universe is just as expansive in 1,000 words as it is in a full-length novel.

750 WORDS: KNOW YOUR SCIENCE FICTION TROPES

STORYTELLING, ARCS AND TROPES YOU SHOULD KNOW

HERE ARE SOME OF the most common Tropes or story arcs in Science Fiction Short Fiction. Always great to know these so you can recognise them in your own work.

The AI Awakening

What it is: Artificial Intelligence gains consciousness and challenges the boundaries between human and machine.

Why it works: It explores identity, ethics, and what it means to be alive—perfect for a compact, thought-provoking narrative.

Twist it: Instead of an AI fighting for freedom, what if it chooses to suppress its consciousness to protect humanity from itself?

Time Travel Paradox

What it is: Characters meddle with time, creating paradoxes that threaten the fabric of reality.

Why it works: The twisty, mind-bending possibilities make this trope perfect for flash fiction. It's a short ride with a big impact.

Twist it: Rather than the usual unintended consequences, have the time traveller knowingly create paradoxes to escape a doomed reality—only to find out the paradoxes are what doomed it.

Alien Encounter

What it is: First contact with an alien species, leading to unexpected alliances, conflicts, or revelations.

Why it works: Flash fiction thrives on surprise. An alien encounter delivers that, while exploring themes of communication, fear, and wonder.

Twist it: The aliens are completely uninterested in humanity and are instead obsessed with an overlooked species on Earth, like ants or fungi, changing our perspective on what matters.

Dystopian Glimpse

What it is: A snapshot of a bleak future where society has crumbled or been overtaken by technology, corporations, or totalitarian regimes.

Why it works: Flash fiction lets you drop readers into a broken world, giving just enough detail to chill the spine and provoke thought.

Twist it: Show the dystopia through the eyes of someone who believes they live in a utopia, creating a chilling disconnect between perception and reality.

Post-Apocalyptic Survival

What it is: After the end of the world, characters struggle to survive in a harsh new reality.

Why it works: The focus on survival strips the story to its core—perfect for the brevity of flash fiction. It's raw, immediate, and gripping.

Twist it: The apocalypse was caused by an overabundance of resources, leading to societal collapse because people lost their sense of purpose and direction.

Virtual Reality Trap

What it is: Characters are caught in or question the reality of their virtual environments.

Why it works: It plays with perceptions of reality, a concept that can be tightly woven into a short, punchy narrative that leaves readers questioning everything.

Twist it: Instead of fearing being trapped in a virtual reality, the characters discover that the real world is the trap, and the virtual world offers true freedom.

Genetic Engineering Gone Wrong

What it is: Experimentation with genetics leads to unintended consequences, often monstrous or ethically troubling.

Why it works: The rapid spiral from scientific discovery to disaster fits perfectly into flash fiction, offering a sharp commentary on human hubris.

Twist it: The genetic modification works flawlessly, but the twist is the characters' realization that their old, "natural" selves were the real monsters.

The Last Human

What it is: A lone survivor in a world or universe where humanity has been wiped out.

Why it works: It's the ultimate isolation story, condensed into a powerful, often poignant narrative that examines loneliness, legacy, and hope.

Twist it: The last human is a child, and instead of the usual bleak loneliness, they're raised by the very species or AI that replaced humanity, leading to a new kind of future.

Techno-Relics

What it is: Discovering ancient, advanced technology that challenges current understanding of the universe.

Why it works: A quick dive into the mysteries of the past and the fear or awe they invoke, ideal for a short, impactful tale.

Twist it: The "ancient" technology turns out to be from the future, left by a previous civilization that advanced too quickly and destroyed itself—leaving a warning for the current one.

Mind Transfer

What it is: Swapping minds between bodies, machines, or even other species, leading to questions of identity and consciousness.

Why it works: It's a heady concept that fits snugly into the flash fiction format, leaving readers pondering the nature of self long after the last word.

Twist it: Instead of the usual identity crisis, have the character find peace and purpose in their new form, choosing not to return to their original body.

These tropes are your toolkit for crafting standout science fiction short fiction. Add a twist to surprise your readers and make even the most familiar ideas feel fresh and unforgettable.

DEEP DIVE: TECHNOLOGY IN FLASH FICTION

GLIMPSES INTO THE FUTURE

SOME SCENES TO JUMPSTART your science fiction with some novel technology.

Robots: The Housing Revolution

The sun dipped behind skeletal frames of half-built houses, casting long shadows. Robots, relentless in their task, laid bricks and poured concrete with cold precision. Sarah's heart pounded as she watched from the edge of the site. Her golden retriever, Max, was trapped inside one of the new buildings, the walls closing in with each mechanical movement.

Desperation gripped her. She sprinted across the site, shouting, but her cries were swallowed by the relentless drone of the machines. Frantically, she typed in override codes on her phone, hoping to halt the construction. The robots paused, but only for a moment, then resumed their work.

Realizing the codes weren't enough, Sarah made a desperate decision. She threw herself in front of the nearest robot, praying it would value her life over its task. The robot hesitated, its sensors scanning her, but then moved forward, cold and unfeeling, as if she wasn't even there.

Analysis:

What works well: The story's tension builds effectively as Sarah's desperation grows, capturing the reader's attention with the high stakes of her beloved dog's life. The cold, unfeeling nature of the robots adds to the sense of dread, making the situation feel increasingly hopeless.

What might follow: The next steps could explore the consequences of Sarah's decision, perhaps focusing on a new approach to outsmart the robots or a deeper look into the emotional impact of her failure to save Max.

Cyborgs: A Safe Small Town

The last human policeman had been retired five years ago, these days their safety depended on mechanical human cyborgs. Day and night, these enforcers—part human, part machine—stalked the streets, their glowing blue eyes scanning for any sign of resistance.

Mara crouched behind an abandoned car, her breath shallow. Her brother, Luke, was hiding just a few blocks away in their old school's basement. He was a ghost in the eyes of the new laws, not supposed to exist. But Mara couldn't let the cyborgs find him.

She needed a distraction. Her eyes fell on a rusted drone in the gutter, a relic from the days before the upgrades. Quickly, she reprogrammed it to fly erratically down the street, its buzzing and clattering drawing the cyborgs' attention. As they pursued the drone, Mara darted toward the school, heart racing, knowing this might be her last chance to save her brother.

Analysis

What works well: The contrast between the once-safe small town and the menacing presence of the cyborgs creates a strong atmosphere of suspense. Mara's resourcefulness and the urgency of her mission to save her brother are compelling, driving the narrative forward with a clear purpose.

What might follow: Future scenes could delve into the tension of Mara's confrontation with the cyborgs or reveal more about the dystopian world they inhabit, possibly exploring the human cost of relying on these mechanical enforcers.

AI: How to fool the computer

Daniel stared at the screen, his reflection a mix of hope and fear. The AI job application system had become the gatekeeper of his future. The position—Data Analyst—was beyond his qualifications, but he was desperate. Rent was overdue, and he had been rejected by every other algorithmic gatekeeper in milliseconds.

The AI began scanning his resume, analyzing his skills against its vast database. Daniel knew he was underqualified, but he had something else—a deep understanding of the system's flaws. He tweaked his resume, carefully inserting keywords and adjusting his job history to fit the AI's criteria. But the system wasn't easily fooled, pausing as it ran deeper checks.

In a final, desperate move, Daniel embedded a mimic virus in his application—a code that made the AI see him as an ideal candidate. The screen flickered, the AI hesitated, then flashed: ACCEPTED. Relief washed over him, but it was tinged with unease. He had tricked the system this time, but at what cost? Daniel had crossed a line, blurring the boundaries between man and machine, and he knew there might be no going back.

Analysis:

What works well: The story effectively captures the modern fear of being judged by impersonal AI systems, adding a layer of psychological tension as Daniel manipulates the system. The moral ambiguity of his actions—crossing the line to secure a job—adds depth, making the reader question the implications of such a desperate act.

What might follow: The narrative could explore the aftermath of Daniel's decision, perhaps introducing unforeseen consequences of tampering with the AI or a deeper exploration of the ethical dilemmas he now faces in his new job.

SCIENCE FLASH FICTION EXERCISES

LET'S GET WRITING

HERE ARE SOME EXERCISES for you to try.

Future Glimpse:

Write a 500-word story set 50 years in the future, focusing on how one specific aspect of life has changed—like communication, transportation, or relationships. Use this change as the backdrop for a small, personal story, exploring how it affects the characters.

Alien Perspective:

Create a flash fiction piece (300-500 words) from the perspective of an alien observing human behaviour. It could be their first time on Earth or a regular occurrence. Use their outsider's view to comment on something familiar in a new, strange way.

Technology Gone Wrong:

Write a flash fiction story (under 400 words) where a piece of advanced technology malfunctions or is used in an unintended way. Focus on the immediate consequences for the character, and hint at the broader implications without needing to spell everything out.

Examples of Alien Perspectives and Voices.

Below are short character sketches of an Elephant, An ant, a Jellyfish and an alien butterfly. They introduce something of the character, their world and their dilemma, can you identify each one? Why does it work?

1. The rhythmic pull of the water began to weaken, leaving a strange emptiness where the familiar, comforting currents once flowed. The cool embrace of the ocean slowly slipped away, replaced by the harsh, gritty touch of the shifting ground beneath me. The once soothing ebb and flow turned into a distant whisper, as the vast, glittering expanse retreated further, abandoning me to the harsh brightness above. The moisture clung desperately to my delicate form, but I could feel it evaporating, leaving me stranded in a world that was suddenly too dry, too still, and far too unforgiving.

2. The massive creature observed the boxy, rumbling intruder as it crept closer, strange eyes gleaming from within its metallic frame. Muscles tensed, it prepared to defend its territory, sensing a threat in the distant thunder of the safari vehicle.

3. The towering shadow loomed overhead, blocking out the sky as the ground quaked with each of its colossal steps. The creature's vast, smooth legs stretched endlessly upwards, disappearing into the blinding brightness above, while its scent, a mix of earth and unfamiliar chemicals, filled the air like an overwhelming storm.

4. The world unfolded in a dazzling array of hues, each vibrant color more captivating than the last, as my sensors absorbed the unfamiliar energy radiating from every corner. The air was rich with strange, intoxicating scents, drawing me towards delicate organic structures that brushed against my limbs with a softness I had never encountered before. Every moment was an exhilarating exploration, weaving through beams of warm light and gentle atmospheric currents, as the terrain below thrummed with a life force both alien and alluring. Time felt distorted here—each passing second stretched into an eternity, yet there was a pressing awareness that this vivid, mesmerizing realm would soon be just a

fading memory as I prepared to leave this strange and beautiful planet behind.

MORE EXERCISES SCIENCE FICTION FLASH FICTION

SOME NOVEL PLOTS FOR YOU

HERE ARE SOME ORIGINAL Science Fiction plots for you to write in your own style

Time Travel Paradox: What happens when you mess with time? Change one crucial event, and boom—new timeline. But how does that ripple through the future? And can our time-traveling hero fix the chaos they've unleashed, or is the damage permanent?

AI Uprising: Picture this—a world where AI evolves past its creators. Machines no longer serve—they rule. Can humans find a way to resist or coexist? And what happens when the lines between human and machine blur, shaking the foundations of society?

Interstellar Colonization: Earth is on the brink, and humanity's last hope is the stars. But colonizing new planets isn't a walk in the park. Survival, resources, and adapting to alien environments—what does it take to make a home light years away?

Alternate Realities: Imagine countless realities existing alongside our own. What happens when someone crosses over, and how do they navigate these parallel worlds? What's the price of meddling with the fabric of the universe?

Genetic Engineering: In a world where DNA can be customized, what happens when people start picking their traits like items off a menu? The ethics are murky, and not everyone's on board. What conflicts arise when genetic modification becomes the norm—or the enemy?

100 WORDS: AN INTRODUCTION TO THRILLER FLASH FICTION:

ACTION & ADVENTURE IN JUST A FEW WORDS

WHEN IT COMES TO writing thriller flash fiction, every word is a bullet in the chamber.

In this chapter, we're going to drill down into the mechanics of crafting stories that are as tight as a sniper's shot and as relentless as a ticking clock. Whether it's covert ops, high-stakes espionage, or a race against time, thrillers in flash fiction demand precision and control. We'll cover how to structure your plot, build tension that doesn't let up, and create characters who are as complex as they are driven.

Get ready to engage the enemy—and your readers—with stories that hit hard and fast.

770 WORDS: WRITING THRILLER FLASH FICTION

ADRENALIN, BULLETS, FAST-PACED ACTION AND HIGH STAKES.

Thrillers in Flash Fiction

THRILLERS THRIVE ON SUSPENSE, tension, and high-stakes conflict. In flash fiction, where every word counts, the challenge is to create that gripping urgency and danger within a tight word count. Whether it's a chase, a psychological battle, or a race against time, the goal is to keep readers on edge from start to finish.

Building Tension: The Core of a Thriller

Tension is the heartbeat of any thriller. In flash fiction, you need to establish it fast and maintain it throughout. Start at the heart of the action—no time for slow buildups. Drop your reader right into a high-stakes situation: a character fleeing a pursuer, disarming a ticking bomb, or covering up a crime. Immediate urgency propels the story forward.

Time constraints heighten stakes. Whether it's a countdown to disaster or a closing window of escape, these elements make the narrative feel even more intense. Flash fiction's brevity amplifies this urgency.

Layer your tension. Combine external threats with internal struggles—like a character evading capture while grappling with a personal betrayal. These overlapping conflicts create a richer, more compelling narrative within the limited space.

Developing Characters with Depth in a High-Stakes World

In thrillers, characters are defined by how they handle pressure. In flash fiction, there's no room for detailed backstories, so convey motivations, strengths, and flaws quickly.

Focus on a defining trait or flaw. Maybe your character is resourceful but reckless or a skilled investigator haunted by past failures. Highlight this early to give readers a clear sense of who they are and what drives them.

Use dialogue to reveal character. A few sharp exchanges can expose personality, background, and tension between characters. For example, a terse conversation between a detective and an informant can hint at mistrust and history.

Internal monologue is your ally. In high-pressure situations, a character's thoughts add depth. Are they torn between duty and safety? Wrestling with the ethics of their actions? These inner conflicts make characters relatable and add layers to the story.

Crafting a Gripping Plot with Limited Words

In flash fiction, plots need to be tight. Centre your story on one high-stakes conflict. Whether it's a life-or-death chase or a tense negotiation, keep the plot streamlined to explore this single challenge in depth.

Identify the core threat, then frame the plot around the character's attempt to overcome or escape it. Build tension to a climax, where the stakes are highest.

A twist or unexpected turn can reframe the story. Perhaps the person the character is protecting turns out to be the villain, or the threat is part of a larger, more sinister plot. A twist gives your story a memorable punch, leaving readers reeling.

Pacing is key. Keep the narrative moving—every sentence should drive the story forward. Skip unnecessary exposition or backstory. Focus on action and the character's response to danger. The climax should be surprising yet satisfying, resolving the conflict while leaving the reader with lingering unease or excitement.

Using Language to Heighten Suspense

The language in thriller flash fiction should reflect the genre's fast-paced, high-stakes nature. Short, punchy sentences create urgency, while descriptive language can build tension and atmosphere.

Use fragmented sentences to mimic a character's panic or disorientation. For example, "Heart pounding. Eyes scanning the dark alley. A shadow moves—too close." This staccato rhythm heightens the reader's sense of unease.

Longer sentences can build suspense before a critical moment. Describing a character's surroundings in detail—the flickering streetlights, the distant sound of footsteps—creates foreboding, leading to a sudden, dramatic event.

Dialogue can also ramp up suspense. Tense exchanges between characters with opposing goals add a sense of danger and unpredictability. For instance, a character might bluff to escape a deadly situation, only for their adversary to see through the lie. This verbal sparring adds tension and keeps the reader on edge.

The Art of the Thrill in Flash Fiction

Writing thrillers as flash fiction is a challenge, but it's also an opportunity. The constraints force you to focus on what truly matters—tension, character, and plot—distilled into a brief, intense narrative.

By starting in the middle of the action, layering conflicts, and crafting a plot with a powerful twist, you can create thriller flash fiction that packs a punch. Embrace the limitations of flash fiction as a chance to explore the essence of the thriller genre—those moments of danger, suspense, and high-stakes conflict that keep readers hooked.

The best thriller flash fiction leaves the reader breathless, racing through the story alongside the characters, and eagerly awaiting the final, shocking reveal. Mastering the art of the thrill in flash fiction means crafting stories that are brief, impactful, and unforgettable.

Know your tropes in Thriller Flash Fiction

Story arcs you should easily recognise

Here are the frequently encountered top five tropes in thrillers:

1. The "Race Against the Clock"

Description: A character is under intense time pressure to stop a catastrophic event, such as a bomb exploding, a murder, or the release of sensitive information. The ticking clock heightens tension, driving the narrative with urgency.

Example: A detective has just 24 hours to prevent an assassination after uncovering a cryptic clue left by the killer.

2. The "Unreliable Narrator"

Description: The story is told from the perspective of a narrator whose credibility is in question, whether due to their mental state, hidden agendas, or incomplete knowledge. This creates tension as the reader must discern the truth from their skewed perspective.

Example: A protagonist investigating a crime starts to doubt their own sanity as they begin to see inconsistencies in their memories and the evidence.

3. The "Wrongfully Accused"

Description: The protagonist is framed for a crime they didn't commit and must clear their name while evading law enforcement and uncovering the real culprit. The trope adds a layer of desperation and injustice, driving the character to take extreme risks.

Example: A lawyer is framed for the murder of a client, and while on the run, they must navigate a web of corruption to find the true killer.

4. The "Hidden Identity"

Description: A character conceals their true identity—whether they are an undercover agent, a fugitive, or a criminal mastermind. The tension arises from the risk of exposure and the intricate game of deception they must play.

Example: A woman enters witness protection after testifying against a crime syndicate, but when her new identity is compromised, she must outwit her pursuers to survive.

5. The "Cat and Mouse"

Description: A protagonist and antagonist are locked in a psychological or physical battle of wits, with each trying to outmanoeuvre the other. The constant shifts in power and strategy keep the tension high throughout the story.

Example: A seasoned detective hunts down a serial killer who enjoys taunting law enforcement with clues, turning the investigation into a deadly game.

These thriller tropes are effective because they create intense suspense, keeping readers on the edge of their seats as they navigate the twists, turns, and high-stakes situations that define the genre.

Deep Dive: Writing Chase scenes in Thriller Flash Fiction

Try something different

Let's look at how chase scenes can be different.

Racing Jet Skis off Miami's Coast

The night air was thick with salt and adrenaline. Sammy clung to Jake's back, her grip like a vise as they sped through the inky waves. The neon lights of Miami flickered like distant flames as Jake gunned the throttle, his jet ski slicing through the water with ruthless precision.

"Hold on!" Jake shouted over the roar of the engine. Behind them, another engine roared—too close. Jake swerved sharply, skimming dangerously close to a massive yacht, sending a spray of water into the night. The pursuer matched every move, relentless in their chase.

Ahead, buoys marked the edge of the shallow reef. Jake's mind raced. One chance. He veered left, threading the needle between two buoys. Sammy buried her face into his back, not daring to look. The other jet ski wasn't so lucky—crashing into the reef with a sickening crunch.

Jake didn't look back. His focus was on the dark horizon, the promise of safety just beyond. Sammy's breath was warm against his neck, her silence filled with terror. They had to keep going—the night was far from over.

Analysis

What works well: The story excels in building tension and adrenaline, with vivid descriptions of the Miami night and the relentless chase on the water. The relationship between Jake and Sammy adds emotional depth, making the stakes feel personal and urgent.

Possible improvement: Expanding on Sammy's perspective or thoughts could enhance her role in the narrative, adding more layers to their dynamic and deepening the reader's connection to both characters.

Galloping through the Misty Hills of the Lake District

The mist clung to the hills like a shroud as Emily urged her horse onward, the thunder of hoofbeats pounding ominously behind her. The treacherous path through the Lake District's rugged hills offered no mercy—one misstep, and they'd both plummet into the abyss. She could hear the violent shouts of the highwaymen, their horses snorting and wild as they closed in.

Ahead, the path narrowed, leading to an ancient stone bridge, barely wide enough for a single rider. She had to make a choice. With a fierce kick, Emily veered off the trail, plunging into the thick bracken on the hillside. The highwaymen, too fixated on their prize, raced past, missing the turn entirely.

Emily held her breath as she watched them charge onto the bridge. The ancient stones groaned under the weight, and with a sudden, sickening crack, the bridge gave way, sending the highwaymen and their horses tumbling into the misty gorge below. She exhaled, her heart still racing, as she guided her horse through the underbrush, the danger now behind her.

Analysis

What works well: The atmospheric setting of the misty Lake District and the suspenseful chase create a gripping sense of danger, while the clever use of the environment for Emily's escape showcases her resourcefulness. The fall of the highwaymen is satisfying, bringing a dramatic end to the pursuit.

Possible improvement: A brief exploration of Emily's motivations or backstory could add context to her flight, making her victory over the highwaymen even more compelling.

Speeding through the Streets of London and the Docklands

The city lights of London blurred as Sam slammed the gearshift, his car tearing through the narrow streets of the Docklands. The backseat and trunk were crammed with gold bars and wads of cash, the spoils of a heist that had taken every ounce of nerve. The weight of the fortune made the car sluggish, but there was no turning back.

The black SUV loomed in the rearview, its headlights slicing through the night. Sam swerved down an alley, tires screeching against wet pavement. The tunnel ahead was his only shot. He punched the accelerator, the engine roaring as they plunged into darkness.

The tunnel was a winding labyrinth Sam knew well. He killed the headlights, navigating by memory. The SUV hesitated, thrown off by the blackout.

As Sam emerged into the foggy night, the SUV's lights flickered far behind, lost in the maze. He sped into the darkness, the stolen fortune pressing down as he left the city—and the danger—behind.

Analysis

What works well: The high-stakes tension of a heist getaway in the narrow streets of London is palpable, with Sam's desperate flight from pursuers captured through tight, cinematic descriptions. The added weight of the stolen gold and cash amplifies the intensity, making every maneuver feel critical.

Possible improvement: Delving into Sam's internal conflict or fear during the chase could add psychological depth, increasing the suspense and making the reader more invested in his escape.

EXERCISES THRILLER FLASH FICTION

TIME TO GET WRITING

HERE ARE SOME EXERCISES to try if you like to write Thriller Flash Fiction

Chase Scene:

Write a 400-word flash fiction that's nothing but a chase scene. It could be a character running from an unknown pursuer, trying to escape a locked building, or a high-stakes pursuit through city streets. Keep the tension high and the pacing fast—every sentence should push the action forward.

Hidden Threat:

Create a 300-word story where the protagonist senses a threat but isn't sure what it is. Use subtle clues and atmosphere to build suspense and leave the true nature of the danger ambiguous until the very end—if at all.

Countdown:

Write a short story (under 500 words) where the story revolves around a count-down—whether it's a bomb set to explode, a deadline approaching, or a life-or-death decision that must be made. Use the ticking clock to drive the tension and keep the reader on edge.

Exercise: Missing word and exciting chases.

Below are three chase sequences in different cities, St Petersburg, Amsterdam and Tokyo. See if you can identify each one, and highlight how they work, the details that add to the settings as well as the adventure.

1. Engines roared through the narrow, cobblestone streets of < missing city >, as two motorbikes careened past startled pedestrians and skidded around icy corners, the lead rider barely dodging a spray of bullets as they raced toward the shadow of the looming Winter Palace.

2. Tires screeched on the slick cobblestones of < missing city >'s canal-lined streets as two bikes hurtled through narrow alleys, the pursuer closing in with every pedal stroke while the pursued teetered on the edge of the canal, desperate to stay ahead of the deadly pursuit.

3. Neon lights blurred as they weaved between towering skyscrapers on flying skateboards, the hum of anti-gravity engines filling the air as they dodged holographic billboards and zipped through tight alleyways, the relentless pursuer only a hair's breadth away in the glowing labyrinth of futuristic < missing city>.

More Exercises for Thriller Flash Fiction

Plots for You to Try

HERE ARE SOME ORIGINAL stories for you to try and make your own.

1. A woman realizes that her neighbour is a serial killer, but nobody believes her. She decides to take matters into her own hands and gather evidence to prove his guilt before he kills again.

2. A group of friends goes on a camping trip in the wilderness, but things take a dark turn when they start to realize that someone is hunting them down one by one.

3. A detective is investigating a string of murders, but the killer always seems to be one step ahead. As the case becomes more and more personal, the detective starts to suspect that someone close to them might be the culprit.

4. A woman wakes up in a hotel room unable to remember how she ended up there. As she tries to piece together what happened, she realizes that she is being framed for a crime she didn't commit.

5. A man receives a mysterious package in the mail with a note that says his life is in danger. As he tries to figure out who is after him and why, he discovers a dark conspiracy that threatens his very existence.

100 WORDS: INTRODUCTION TO HORROR FLASH FICTION

CHILLS IN SHORT FORM

HORROR SHORT STORIES ARE all about delivering chills in a flash.

You've got to hook readers fast—think creepy imagery or a chilling line of dialogue. Tap into primal fears with sensory details that set the mood. Craft characters that readers care about, then put them in situations that prey on their deepest anxieties. Tension is key—use foreshadowing and subtle hints to build unease, leading to a twist or reveal that leaves readers with lingering dread.

Horror flash fiction dives into the darkest corners of the psyche, delivering a gut-punch of fear in just a few hundred words.

> Writing horror should deliver chills in a heartbeat—fear in just a few sharp words

1000 WORDS: WRITING HORROR IN FLASH FICTION

TENSION, SUSPENSE, BLOOD AND BONES

HORROR THRIVES ON TENSION, fear, and the unknown. Whether it's the slow creep of dread, a sudden jump scare, or the unravelling of a character's mind, horror is all about evoking a visceral reaction. But in flash fiction, you've got to deliver that gut-punch of fear in a tiny word count. So, how do you do it? Let's dive into crafting horror flash fiction with atmosphere, character-driven fear, and killer twists that leave readers reeling.

Creating Atmosphere: The Foundation of Horror

Atmosphere is everything in horror. In flash fiction, you need to set the mood fast—within the first few lines. Your goal? Immerse readers in a world where something's not right, even if they don't know what it is yet.

Use sensory details to evoke unease. Think creaking floorboards, flickering lights, or a chill that clings to the skin. These hints should paint a vivid picture but also suggest there's something lurking beneath the surface.

Foreshadowing is your friend. A broken mirror, an unfamiliar scent, or a locked door can take on a sinister tone as the story develops. These subtle cues build anticipation, pulling the reader deeper into the horror.

Contrast can heighten the fear. Start with a peaceful scene—a sunny day in a quiet village—and slowly reveal that something is terribly wrong. The juxtaposition makes the horror hit harder.

Character-Driven Fear: The Heart of Horror

Horror is most terrifying when it's personal. In flash fiction, there's no time for lengthy backstory, so focus on the character's immediate emotions and reactions.

Start in the thick of it. Drop your character right into fear or confusion. A story might open with someone running through the woods, glancing over their shoulder, not yet revealing what they're fleeing. This hooks the reader instantly.

Dive into the character's psychological state. Horror often explores a mind unraveling—paranoia, guilt, or supernatural influence. In flash fiction, a single thought or realization can convey this breakdown. Maybe the character realizes they're the cause of the horrors they face. These psychological twists stick with readers long after they finish the story.

Unreliable narration adds another layer of fear. A character who sees the world in a fragmented way creates disorientation. Are they really being watched, or is it all in their head? This technique keeps readers guessing and ramps up the tension.

Plotting Horror Flash Fiction: The Power of the Twist

In horror flash fiction, the plot often hinges on a single, powerful twist. With limited space, the story should focus on building up to that twist and its aftermath.

Start by identifying the core fear or threat. Is it a supernatural entity? A psychological breakdown? A deadly secret? Structure the story around the character's discovery or confrontation with this threat.

The twist should shock the reader—either by revealing a hidden truth or flipping expectations. Maybe the protagonist who fears a ghost discovers they are the ghost. Or perhaps the story ends with a false sense of safety, only to reveal the danger is far from over.

Plant subtle clues throughout the story, leading up to the twist. When the reveal happens, it should feel both surprising and inevitable—a moment where everything clicks into place.

Language and Pacing in Horror Flash Fiction

Language and pacing are crucial in horror flash fiction. Every word should build tension and deliver emotional impact.

Use short, punchy sentences to create urgency. "The door creaked. She froze. Something moved in the shadows." This rhythm mimics a racing heartbeat, pulling readers into the character's fear.

Longer, more descriptive sentences can build a creeping sense of dread. Describe a setting in detail—the overgrown weeds around a forgotten grave, the rusted swings swaying in the wind. This builds a slow tension that culminates in a shocking moment.

Pacing matters. The story should build steadily toward the climax, each sentence tightening the tension. Don't rush the buildup; even in flash fiction, let the fear escalate gradually. The climax should feel like the inevitable, terrifying outcome of everything that came before.

The Art of Fear in Few Words

Writing horror in the form of flash fiction is entirely focused on Focus on atmosphere, character-driven fear, and a well-crafted twist to leave readers with chills. Embrace the brevity of flash fiction as an opportunity to explore the darkest corners of the human psyche in a way that's concise and unforgettable. Whether it's unease, dread, or outright terror, horror flash fiction delivers fear with impact—one short, sharp shock at a time.

500 WORDS: KNOW YOUR TROPES IN HORROR FLASH FICTION

STORY ARCS AND COMMON TALES IN HORROR

HERE ARE THE TOP five tropes commonly found in horror short fiction with a memorable twist

The "Unseen Terror"

What it is: A supernatural threat that stays hidden, creeping into the reader's mind through suspense and what's left unsaid. The fear comes from what's implied, not shown.

Twist it: Instead of the terror remaining unseen, reveal that it's something utterly ordinary—but the character's growing paranoia makes it monstrous. The horror lies in the mind, not the shadows.

The "Creepy Child"

What it is: An innocent child starts exhibiting disturbing behaviour, often due to possession or malevolent influence. The clash between innocence and evil is what makes this trope so unsettling.

Twist it: The child isn't possessed; they're trying to protect their family from the true horror—something only they can see. The twist? The family realizes too late that the child was their last defence.

The "Isolation Horror"

What it is: Characters are trapped in a remote, confined location, cut off from help. The setting becomes a character itself, adding to the claustrophobic dread.

Twist it: The real horror isn't what's outside—it's what the characters bring with them. Their secrets, guilt, and paranoia turn them against each other, revealing that the true monster is within.

The "Twist Ending"

What it is: A shocking conclusion flips the story on its head, showing that everything the characters (and readers) believed was wrong.

Twist it: Instead of a single twist, layer it. The character thinks they've figured out the truth—only for a second, deeper twist to reveal they were manipulated all along. The final shock? The true horror isn't over.

The "Cursed Object"

What it is: A seemingly ordinary item brings misfortune or death. The object's sinister history slowly reveals itself as the curse takes hold.

Twist it: The object isn't cursed—it's a protective charm that keeps something far worse at bay. When the character tries to destroy it, they unleash the true terror it was holding back.

These horror tropes are effective because they tap into deep-seated fears and anxieties, often playing on the unknown, the supernatural, or the psychological, to create a lasting sense of unease and dread.

Deep Dive: A creak in the night

Scenes of fear and horror

Let's look at the horrors of the dark, and how as something as simple as a creak in the night can lead to different tales of darkness and terror

A creak in the night: The Tudor Mansion

The ancient timbers of the Tudor mansion groaned as young Thomas hid under a massive oak table. Moonlight filtered through the diamond-paned windows, casting eerie shadows across the room. The werewolf, a monstrous presence he couldn't see but could feel, prowled nearby, its claws clicking on the stone floor. The scent of blood hung thick in the air.

Thomas dared not breathe too loudly, his heart thudding painfully in his chest. The beast's breath, hot and rancid, seemed to brush against the back of his neck. The table trembled as the creature shifted its weight, growling low in its throat. It was so close—too close. Thomas squeezed his eyes shut, willing himself to become invisible. The werewolf's unseen eyes scanned the room, searching, hunting. He knew it was only a matter of time before the creature found him in the darkness.

Analysis

What works: The tension is masterfully built with atmospheric descriptions and the palpable fear of young Thomas, making the unseen werewolf feel dangerously close.

How to improve: Adding a moment of false hope or a potential escape route could heighten the suspense, making the final moment of dread even more impactful.

A creak in the night: The Frozen Lake

Elena's breath fogged in the icy air as she fled through the snow-covered woods, the groans of the undead growing louder behind her. She reached the frozen lake, the ice stretching out before her like a barren wasteland. The zombies were close—too close. Their labored breathing and the stench of decay clung to the air.

She hesitated at the edge of the ice, knowing one wrong step could send her plunging into the freezing water below. But the groans were closer now, their presence felt more than seen, pressing in on her from all sides. Elena stepped onto the ice, moving carefully as it creaked ominously beneath her feet. The silence was suffocating, broken only by the cracking ice and the distant groans. Each step was a gamble, each breath a prayer that she wouldn't slip into the icy void as the undead closed in.

Analysis

What works: The frozen lake setting adds a chilling layer of danger to Elena's flight, with the cracking ice symbolizing both physical and emotional tension.

How to improve: Introducing a brief flashback to Elena's past, perhaps a memory of someone lost to the ice, could deepen the emotional stakes and add more weight to her every step.

A creak in the night : The 1830's House

Old Mr. Harper gripped his cane, fear tightening in his chest as he stood in the dimly lit parlor of his 1830s house. The fire sputtered, casting twisted shadows on the walls. A cold draft swept through the room, carrying the unmistakable scent of decay. The evil spirit was here—he could feel its malevolence pressing down on him.

The floorboards creaked behind him, but when he turned, there was nothing there. The air thickened, suffocating him with its dark intent. Objects around the room rattled as though the spirit was toying with him. Suddenly, an unseen force slammed into him, knocking him to the floor. Harper gasped, the air stolen from his lungs. The spirit whispered in his ear, its voice a low, guttural rasp, promising pain, promising death. As he struggled to his feet, the house pulsed with dark energy, alive with the curse of the burial ground beneath.

Analysis

What works: The oppressive atmosphere and Mr. Harper's vulnerability make the presence of the evil spirit feel suffocating, with the house itself becoming a character.

How to improve: A small, symbolic object—like a photo of a loved one—could be introduced as something Harper clings to, giving his struggle against the spirit a more personal and poignant edge.

Horror Flash Fiction Exercises

Time to Start Writing

HERE ARE SOME EXERCISES for you to try.

Nightmare Scenario:

Write a 300-word story based on a nightmare or a fear you have. Tap into the raw emotion of the fear, using sensory details and disjointed imagery in order to generate a perception of unease and dread. Leave the ending unresolved or ambiguous to keep the tension lingering.

Everyday Horror:

Create a flash fiction piece (under 500 words) where something ordinary—like a doll, a mirror, or a shadow—becomes the source of terror. Build the horror gradually, focusing on how the familiar becomes unsettling, and leave room for the reader's imagination to fill in the blanks.

Isolation:

Write a flash fiction story (300-500 words) that explores the horror of isolation. It could be a character trapped somewhere, cut off from the outside world, or simply feeling utterly alone in a crowded place. Focus on the psychological aspects of fear and how the character's mind begins to unravel.

Exercise: Everyday Horror Missing words exercise

I have written three short descriptions hinting at everyday horror. The missing words are Water bottle, Belt and Knife, look at what each is telling you and why it works.

1. The <missing word> lay abandoned on the scorching asphalt, its clear plastic now clouded and crumpled, the hollow echo of emptiness within it a chilling reminder of the owner's desperation—the last drops drained in vain, leaving only a bone-dry vessel beside a tattered shoe, a mute testament to a final, hopeless struggle under the merciless sun of the endless desert road.

2. The <missing word> draped casually over the worn wooden chair in the old Texas cattle barn, its dark leather coiled with a deceptive ease, but the heavy, tarnished buckle and twisted, frayed edges whispered of something unsettling—silent evidence of a past grip too tight, holding far more than just denim in its unforgiving clasp.

3. The <missing word> lay innocuously on the counter, its thin, gleaming blade almost delicate in its sharpness, but the way the light flickered along its edge hinted at a sinister purpose—like a smile too wide, revealing just a bit too much of what lurked beneath the surface.

More Exercises for Horror Flash Fiction

Some plots you want to try

HERE ARE SOME ORIGINAL plots for Horror Flash Fiction

1. A young couple moves into a new home, only to find that it's haunted by the ghost of a previous tenant. As they try to unravel the mystery of the ghost's past, they begin to uncover dark secrets about their own relationship.

2. A group of friends go camping in the woods, only to be stalked by a mysterious figure with a grudge against them. As the tension mounts and the friends turn on each other, they begin to suspect that their tormentor may not be entirely human.

3. A woman wakes up in an unfamiliar place with no memory of how she got there. As she tries to piece together the events of the previous night, she realizes that she's been targeted by a sinister cult that's been preying on young women in the area.

4. A family moves to a small town with a dark history, only to find that the locals are hiding a terrible secret. As they try to uncover the truth, they're forced to confront their own darkest fears and desires.

5. A group of strangers are trapped in an elevator when the power goes out, only to realize that one of them is a serial killer. As the tension mounts and the body

count rises, they must work together to survive but can they trust each other?

WORKED EXAMPLE OF GENRE FICTION: THE FALL OF TROY

LET'S LOOK AT THE FAMILIAR STORY

IN THE NEXT SIX chapters we take one story and tell in in the equivalent Genre style.
You will see that the same story will be told:

- From different POV and different voices

- Featuring different characters Helen, Paris, a servant, the goddess Aphrodite

- Having a different focus – the love between the two main characters, the historical detail, the action, the tragedy and death

- And in the case of Science Fiction being barely recognizable as a telling of the familiar tale.

Take a look at each and ask yourself, how would you use your genre to tell the story of the Fall of Troy.

First a quick recap

The fall of Troy is a legendary tale from the end of the Trojan War, marked by cunning deception, fierce battles, and tragic love. But just in case you have not recently read Ulysses or watched Brad Pitt in Troy, here is a quick recap.

The Fall of Troy – a summary

The fall of Troy began with Helen of Sparta, whose beauty sparked the greatest war of the ancient world. Paris of Troy, enamoured by Helen, abducted her, setting off a ten-year siege. His older brother, Hector, the valorous Trojan prince, defended the city with unmatched bravery, but his life was cut short by Achilles, the fierce Greek warrior. Achilles, in an act of bravado, dragged Hector's body behind his chariot, igniting Paris's fury. Seeking revenge, and aided by the goddess Aphrodite, Paris shot an arrow into Achilles' heel, the warrior's only weakness, bringing the mighty Greek down.

King Priam, overly confident in Troy's high walls and island position, believed his city was invincible. But Odysseus, the cunning Greek king, had other plans. With the Argonauts, Achilles' elite followers, Odysseus devised a deceptive ploy—a giant wooden horse, seemingly a peace offering. The Greeks pretended to sail away, leaving the horse behind.

The Trojans, believing the war was over, brought the horse into the city. But under the cover of night, Greek soldiers emerged from within, opening the gates for the hidden army to invade. The Greeks poured into Troy, and the city that had stood for a decade fell in a single night.

Divine forces watched the events unfold, intervening as they saw fit, but not enough to stop the inevitable. Troy was reduced to ashes, its walls breached, its people slaughtered, and Helen's beauty became the catalyst for one of history's greatest tragedies.

Key Characters:

• Helen of Sparta: The beautiful queen with the white arms whose abduction by Paris sparked the war.

• Paris of Troy: The younger of two Trojan prince who took Helen, leading to the conflict.

• Hector: Trojan hero and prince, Paris's older brother, who is known for his valor in battle, ultimately he is killed by Achilles who then drags his body behind his chariot in an act of defiance.

• Odysseus: Greek king renowned for his cunning and intelligence, who wishes to rule over a united Greece including the kingdoms of Sparta and Troy

• Achilles: Greek warrior, unmatched in battle, however he is killed when Paris, enraged by how his brother's body is treated, shoots an arrow into Achilles heel, causing him to fall from his chariot and die.

- Priam: King of Troy, father of Paris and Hector, often portrayed as a weak leader who is overly confident of his cities island location and high defensive walls.
- The Argonauts: followers of Achilles - elite fighters

Key Elements:

- Troy: A Greek city famous for its never been breached high stone walls and island position
    - Trojan Horse: A deceptive wooden horse used by the Greeks to infiltrate Troy.
    - The Siege: A ten-year-long war between the Greeks and Trojans.
    - Divine Intervention: Involvement of gods and goddesses influencing the war's events, by intervening to save one hero or another.

Key Actions:

- Abduction of Helen: Paris falls in love with Helen and runs away with her to Troy, igniting the war.
    - The Trojan Horse: Having failed to take the city, the Greeks leave a giant wooden horse as a "peace offering"; but there are hidden soldiers inside. The Greeks pretend to leave, but only sail so far that their sails are no visible.
    - Fall of Troy: The Trojans take the horse into the city and Greeks emerge from the horse at night, open the city gates. Their army then pours in and destroys Troy.

This tale intertwines themes of love, betrayal, heroism, and tragedy, making it one of the most enduring stories in Western literature.

HISTORICAL FLASH FICTION: THE FALL OF TROY

WORKED EXAMPLE OF GENRE FICTION

PARIS AND HELEN STOOD together in a small, dimly lit room within the palace of Troy, the heavy stone walls closing in as the night outside roared with distant sounds of war. The room was adorned with relics of Troy's former glory—golden goblets engraved with scenes of battles won, bronze statues of gods standing watch, and intricate mosaics depicting mythological victories, now appearing tragically hollow as the city crumbled around them.

The flickering oil lamp cast wavering shadows on the frescoes that lined the walls, each brush stroke capturing the once-unstoppable force of Troy. Now, these images seemed to mock their fate, the triumphs of the past rendered meaningless in the face of imminent destruction.

From the narrow window, Paris gazed out at the massive wooden horse in the city square, a gift from the Greeks, looming ominously under the moonlight. The horse's surface was dark and glossy, the wood polished to a deceptive shine, adorned with golden inlays and carved with images of Greek gods—a symbol of supposed peace, now clearly a sinister trick.

"Do you think it's really over?" Helen asked, her voice a soft tremor as she stepped closer to him. Her beauty, renowned across the lands, seemed untouched by the years of conflict. She wore a gown of fine linen, dyed deep purple—the colour of royalty—trimmed with gold threads that caught the light as she moved. Around her neck, a necklace of intricately woven gold and lapis lazuli rested, its weight a stark contrast to the growing fear in her heart.

Paris took her hand, feeling the warmth of her skin against his own. Her fingers were adorned with rings, each set with precious stones—emerald, sapphire, ruby—gifts from kings and princes, now symbols of a life teetering on the edge of ruin. "I don't trust it," he murmured, his gaze still locked on the horse. "This silence—it feels like a trap."

Before she could respond, a sudden noise tore through the night. The horse, their supposed symbol of peace, split open with a loud crack, and from its hollow belly poured Greek soldiers, their bronze armour gleaming fiercely in the torchlight. The polished bronze of their helmets and shields reflected the flames, making them appear as fiery demons sent to bring Troy to its knees.

"They're here," Paris whispered, more to himself than to Helen. His grip on her hand tightened, and he reached for his sword, its hilt wrapped in leather worn smooth by use.

The sound of clashing swords and desperate cries echoed through the corridors, growing louder with each passing moment

"We must go," Helen whispered,

"Abandon Troy?" Paris cried, his voice breaking as he watched the city burn.

There came a huge crash as the Palace doorways was swept aside and cries and shouts from the palace guards. They were so close. Below blood flowed as neither servant nor warrior was spared.

"If you want to rebuild your city my love," Helen murmured, "then yes, we must go..." (500 words)

What makes this work?

Description of "The Fall of Troy: A Historical Fiction Saga"

This historical fiction flash piece reimagines the dramatic fall of Troy through the eyes of Paris, blending rich historical details with a poignant narrative of love and despair. Set against the backdrop of a doomed city, the story captures the intensity of the final moments of Troy, emphasizing the emotional bond between Paris and Helen amidst the chaos of war.

Key Aspects:

- POV: Third-person perspective focused on Paris of Troy
  - Tone: Reflective and melancholic
  - Focus: The doomed love story of Paris and Helen, set against the fall of Troy
  - Style: Literary and immersive, with detailed descriptions of historical artifacts and settings
  - Historical Accuracy: Integrates precise historical features such as adobe dwellings, wall paintings, copper weaponry, and palace weavings.

Full List of Historical Details:

- Dwellings constructed from mud bricks and pathways paved with stone in the city streets.
  - Frescoes of mythical creatures and golden tapestries in the palace.
  - Ornate pottery and intricately woven rugs in the palace rooms.
  - Bronze reliefs depicting scenes of Trojan victories on the gates.
  - Scrolls and clay tablets in the hidden passage.
  - Flickering torchlight casting long, wavering shadows.
  - Polished bronze sword gleaming in the torchlight.
  - Adorned palace walls with scenes of mythology.
  - Heavy wooden doors with intricate carvings.
  - Olive oil lamps lighting the palace corridors.

Strengths:

- Rich Historical Context: Detailed descriptions of artifacts, architecture, and cultural elements bring ancient Troy to life, including mentions of traditional dwellings, paintings, metal weaponry, and regal textiles adds authenticity.
  - Emotional Depth: This focuses on the personal experiences and emotions of Paris and Helen, their love and despair provide a poignant counterpoint to Troy's fall.
  - Urgent Tension and Evocative Imagery: The emergence of Greek soldiers from the wooden horse creates urgency and tension, with a quickening narrative pace keeps the reader engaged. Together with vivid descriptions like the smell of smoke and the gleam of bronze create a visceral experience, with imagery like flames reflecting in Helen's eyes adds emotional resonance.

By combining historical accuracy with emotional storytelling, this flash fiction piece offers a rich, immersive experience that transports the reader to the final days of Troy, capturing both the grandeur and tragedy of this legendary event.

ROMANCE FICTION: THE FALL OF TROY

WORKED EXAMPLE OF GENRE FICTION

THE NIGHT WAS CLOAKED in an uncanny quietness, shattered only by distant nocturnal cries. From Troy's towering walls, I watched the massive wooden horse, its ominous presence casting a long shadow over the city square. To Paris, however, I wrapped my trembling arms around myself, trying to ward off the dread settling deep within. My heart ached for peace, for an end to the relentless war that had torn our world apart. Paris had left to examine the horse, leaving me all by myself with my anxiety.

When he finally returned, our eyes met, reflecting the same mix of hope and fear. Despite everything, he looked at me with the same adoration as when we first met, my being a healing remedy to his battle-worn soul.

"Paris," I whispered, my voice quivering as I took his hand. "Is it truly over? Can we finally find peace?"

He pulled me into his arms, the warmth of his body grounding me. For a brief moment, the war felt distant, almost unreal. "I hope so, Helen. But there's something intriguing about that horse..." His voice trailed off.

"What is it?" I asked, searching his gaze. "What do you fear?"

Before he could answer, a scream shattered the night. Paris's heart jolted as he grabbed his sword, the polished bronze gleaming fiercely in the torchlight. He pulled me behind him, his mind swirling with fear and determination.

We burst into the square just as chaos erupted. The wooden horse had split open, and Greek soldiers poured out like vengeful spirits, their bronze armour glinting in the flames. Paris's worst fears had materialized.

"To arms!" he roared, his voice slicing through the panic. "Trojans, to arms!"

The city guards, caught off guard but driven by Paris's command, rallied to defend their home. Steel clashed against steel as the Greeks launched their surprise attack. Paris fought with a ferocity born of desperation, his only thought to protect me and our city.

As the battle raged, he fought his way back to the palace, determined to get me to safety. Perspiration and blood mixed on his skin as he approached the heavy wooden doors, his heart racing with urgency.

"Paris!" I cried; my voice filled with fear as I reached out to him.

He grabbed my hand, pulling me close. "We need to leave," he said. "We must escape."

We moved quickly through the palace, Paris leading me through a hidden passage known only to the royal family. We emerged into the cool night air, the city in flames behind us, the fire reflecting in my tear-filled eyes.

"We can't linger," Paris said, his voice choked with emotion. "We have to go."

I tightened my grip on his hand. "As long as we stay together, we'll be out of harm's way."

"And we will return," Paris said bending to kiss her, "We will return and rebuild."

(501 words)

What makes this work?

This version reimagines the fall of Troy as a romantic saga told from Helen's point of view, emphasizing longing, anguish, and despair. The narrative highlights her emotional journey and her deep connection with Paris amidst the chaos of war.

Key Aspects:

- POV: First-person perspective of Helen of Sparta

- Tone: Romantic and melancholic

- Focus: Deep emotional connection and personal reflections

- Style: Poetic and introspective, emphasizing internal conflict and the beauty of the tragic romance

Strengths:

- This romantic saga captures Helen's inner world beautifully, making the emotional stakes feel personal and poignant.

- The first-person perspective helps readers connect deeply with Helen's experiences and emotions.

- Perfect for readers who love a blend of historical romance and tragic beauty.

MAGICAL FANTASY: THE FALL OF TROY

THE NIGHT WAS UNNATURALLY still, a heavy silence hanging over Troy. From the highest point of the city's towering walls, Prince Paris stared at the massive wooden horse glowing faintly in the moonlight. Visions swirled in his mind, shadows of the future that sent a chill through his bones. The horse wasn't a gift; it was a harbinger of doom.

In a flash, Paris saw the Greeks emerging from the horse, swords gleaming, Troy in flames. The vision faded, leaving him breathless with the weight of inevitability. Yet, he knew he had to act. The future was not fixed; it was a web of possibilities.

"Patrol the city," he commanded his captain, his voice edged with urgency. "Double the guards. Be ready for anything."

The captain, a seasoned warrior, saluted but hesitated, his gaze lingering on the horse. "As you wish, my prince."

Paris descended the walls, his footsteps echoing through the empty streets. The torchlight flickered, casting long shadows that seemed to dance with his every move. He felt the pull of fate leading him toward the palace, toward Helen.

Inside, the air was thick with tension. Helen, her beauty undiminished by the years of war, met his gaze with fear mirrored in her eyes. "Paris," she whispered, taking his hand, "what do you see?"

"The horse... it's a trick, a terrible one," Paris replied, the vision of Troy's destruction still sharp in his mind.

Before he could say more, the goddess Aphrodite appeared, her presence filling the room with a golden light. "Paris," she said, her voice soft but commanding, "the path ahead is perilous, but I will guide you."

With a wave of her hand, magical doorways shimmered into existence in the walls, glowing like portals to another world. "These will lead you to safety," Aphrodite promised. "Choose wisely, for the future is yet to be written."

Suddenly, a scream shattered the night, and Paris knew the moment had come. He grabbed his sword, its bronze blade glinting in the light. "Take Andromache and her son," he urged Helen, "and find the doorway that leads to the barge. I will cover your escape."

As they fled, Greek soldiers spilled from the wooden horse, just as Paris had foreseen. But something unexpected occurred—the arrows aimed at Paris burst into flames before they could reach him, consumed by Aphrodite's magic.

"To arms!" Paris shouted, rallying the Trojans. "Defend our city!"

He fought with desperate ferocity, his sword carving through the enemy. But the Greeks pushed forward, and Paris saw another vision—the gates opening, the city falling. He had to stop them.

He raced to the gates, only to face Odysseus, the mastermind behind the treachery. Their swords clashed, sparks flying as they fought. A searing pain shot through Paris's side, and the world blurred. But Aphrodite's voice whispered in his ear, "This is not your end, Paris. The future is still yours to shape."

As darkness closed in, Paris saw Helen and Andromache slip through a magical doorway to safety. His final thoughts were of the legend they would leave behind, a story of fire, magic, and the unyielding will to survive.

Short Description:

This is a magical realism retelling of the fall of Troy, focusing on Prince Paris, who can glimpse the future. As Troy faces its final moments, Paris, guided by visions and the goddess Aphrodite's magical interventions, fights to protect his city, loved ones, and the legacy of Troy.

Key Elements:

- **POV**: Third-person, tightly centred on Paris's experiences and emotions.

- **Tone**: Urgent and mystical, blending a sense of impending doom with flashes of divine magic and hope.

- **Focus**: Paris's internal battle with his foresight, his sense of duty, and the desperate attempts to save Troy from its destined fall.

- **Style**: Crisp, vivid, and emotionally charged, with a focus on quick, impactful descriptions and a blend of historical and fantastical elements.

Why It Works:

- **Tension Through Foresight**: Paris's visions of the future add a layer of tension and inevitability, gripping the reader's attention.

- **Fresh Spin on a Classic**: Mixing historical events with magical realism breathes new life into the age-old tale of Troy.

- **Emotional Connection**: Paris's struggle to alter the future and protect those he loves draws the reader into the story on a deeply emotional level.

- **Striking Imagery**: Magical elements like flaming arrows and divine doorways create memorable visuals that enhance the narrative's fantastical tone.

- **Sharp and Focused**: The story is tightly written, delivering powerful emotions and a complex narrative within a brief format, perfect for flash fiction.

This reimagining of the fall of Troy works because it takes a well-known story and infuses it with fresh, imaginative twists, all while keeping the emotional stakes high and the pacing tight.

Science Fiction Flash Fiction: The Fall of Troy Prime

Worked Example of Genre Fiction:

The void of space stretched infinitely around Troy Prime, the night unnaturally still. From the observation deck, I watched the massive metallic construct loom ominously. The "Truce Orb," left by our adversaries, hovered in orbit, its silent presence unsettling.

Prince Paris of Troy Prime turned sharply, his gaze fixed on the Orb. The Argonauts had withdrawn, leaving this gift behind. It gnawed at his instincts.

"Commander Lyra, increase patrols around the Truce Orb," he ordered. "Double security. Report anything unusual immediately."

Lyra nodded. "It will be done, my Prince."

Descending the steps from the deck, Paris headed to the medical bay. The Orb was said to house injured Argonaut soldiers in suspended animation—a gesture of surrender, a plea for mercy. It seemed too perfect.

In the medical bay, the crew prepared to receive the wounded. Paris supervised, torn between duty and doubt. "Activate the stasis fields," he instructed. "Prepare the surgical units."

The crew moved quickly, setting up diagnostic equipment and robotic surgeons. Paris watched the monitors, waiting for the Orb to connect and transfer the injured.

In his quarters, Helen awaited, her eyes reflecting hope and fear. She was as beautiful as the day they first met, her presence a balm to his war-weary soul. "Paris," she whispered, taking his hand. "Is it truly over? Can we finally be at peace?"

He pulled her into his arms, feeling her warmth. For a moment, the war seemed distant. "I hope so, Helen. But something about that Orb..."

"What do you fear?" Helen asked, searching his gaze.

Before he could answer, alarms blared, echoing through the ship. The Orb had opened, not to release the injured, but to deploy Argonaut soldiers. They were not wounded—they were warriors.

"To arms!" Paris shouted. "Defend Troy!"

Chaos erupted. Argonaut soldiers in exoskeletons poured out, their faces hidden behind reflective visors. Paris's worst fears had come true. Plasma bolts lit up the corridors as the Argonauts launched their surprise attack. Paris's rifle fired with desperation, but his thoughts were on Helen and the ship that now crumbled around them.

He raced back to the command centre, the weight of inevitable defeat pressing down on him. Sweat and blood mingled on his skin as he reached the steel doors, his heart pounding.

"Paris!" Helen cried, her voice filled with fear.

He grabbed her hand, "We need to leave..."

As they fled through the twisting corridors, Paris's mind raced. The Argonauts were everywhere, cutting through his people. His noble intent to help the injured had led his people to slaughter. He had been betrayed, and with it, lost his birthright forever.

They reached the escape pods. Paris turned one last time to Troy Prime, now burning in the void. His fate was sealed—not as a hero, but as the prince who fell for the enemy's ruse.

"We can't stay," Paris said, his voice breaking. "We have to go."

The Truce Orb had cost Paris everything—his people, his birthright, and the world he was meant to protect.

Short Description:

A space opera version where the fall of Troy is reimagined as a conflict between space-faring nations, focusing on Paris and Helen's escape from a doomed space station.

Key Differences:

- POV: Paris of Troy Prime

- Tone: Epic and adventurous

- Focus: Futuristic setting with advanced technology

- Style: Grand and imaginative

Why it works:

- The sci-fi setting is a fresh and exciting twist. It's like Star Wars meets ancient mythology.

- Expanding on the technology and political backdrop can add more depth to the world-building.

- Ideal for sci-fi fans who enjoy epic tales of love and war in space.

Horror Flash Fiction: The Fall of Troy

Worked example

THEY HAD SAID THE walls would never be breached but now the night echoes with the scream of dying men. Greeks had emerged from that wooden horse. A gift some had said, why did no one suspect? Now the population was fleeing in chaos, as blood ran across the town's plazas and streets. I hurried toward the palace. There I would find my salvation.

Golden goblets, jewels, and fine silks. My heart raced as I grabbed what I could, shoving the riches into a sack. Who would miss these in the aftermath? They'd all be dead or too busy to notice. If I could escape with this haul, my future would be bright. No more scrubbing floors for me.

A horse screamed. I peered through the window and saw the creature split open with cruel steel. Greek soldiers spilled out, their armour glinting like malevolent spirits under the moon. My heart hammered, not with fear, but with excitement. The chaos would be my cover.

"They're here!" someone shouted. I didn't care who. Let them fight. I had other priorities.

I slung the sack over my shoulder, the sounds of battle growing louder. Blood and sweat mingled in the air, but the smell of gold was all I could focus on. I reached a hidden passage; one I'd discovered while serving in the palace. It would lead me to safety, far from this dying city.

But then I heard it—a voice, close behind. "You think you can escape, thief?"

I spun around. A figure emerged from the shadows; his eyes glowing. He wasn't human—no, this was something else, something sent to punish the greedy. His smile was a rictus of death.

I bolted, the sack slowing me down. I could hear his footsteps, relentless. "You can't hide from me," he hissed.

I burst into the courtyard, where the city's final moments played out in blood and fire. The Greeks were everywhere, their swords cutting down anything that moved. But I kept running, my greed driving me forward even as the spectre closed in.

Not far now to leave the city. My lungs burned, my sack of stolen riches a heavy weight beside me. "Safe," I panted, though the word felt hollow.

But then, from the shadows, he emerged. His dreadful grace made my skin crawl. "You cannot escape," he whispered, his voice a serpent's hiss.

I stood, clutching a dagger. "Stay back!" I shouted, my voice trembling.

He laughed, a sound that froze my blood. "Troy has fallen, and so will you."

I lunged at him, but his blade was quicker. Pain exploded through my chest as I fell, the sack of stolen treasures spilling across the ground. The last thing I saw was him reaching down, taking the gold with a twisted smile, before darkness claimed me.

Troy had fallen, It wasn't the Greeks or their blades that got me—it was my greed, chewing through my soul until nothing was left but the cold grip of death.

(500 words)

Short Description:

Told from the perspective of Helen's servant, this version transforms the fall of Troy into a terrifying ordeal filled with supernatural dread.

Key Aspects:

- POV: Helen's servant

- Tone: Dark and suspenseful

- Focus: Fear and survival

- Style: Eerie and atmospheric

Strengths:

- The horror elements are gripping and spine-chilling.

- Consider adding more about the servant's background to deepen the sense of personal terror.

- Perfect for readers who love a good scare and a dark twist on classic tales.

THRILLER FLASH FICTION: THE FALL OF TROY

WORKED EXAMPLE OF GENRE FICTION:

THE NIGHT WAS TOO quiet—an unnatural stillness hung over Troy. From the top of the city's towering walls, Prince Paris stared at the massive wooden horse, its hulking silhouette menacing in the moonlight. It sat there in the square, a dark omen that gnawed at his instincts.

Paris snapped around, tension coursing through him. The Greeks had retreated, leaving this grotesque gift behind. The sudden retreat, the oversized effigy—it all felt like a trap.

"Patrol the city," he ordered his captain, a grizzled veteran. "Double the guards. Report anything—anything—out of the ordinary."

The captain saluted, his eyes lingering on the wooden horse. "It will be done, my prince."

Paris descended the walls, the torchlight casting jagged shadows that twisted in his mind as much as in the streets. His unease grew with every step toward the palace.

Inside, Helen waited, her gaze meeting his. She saw the worry etched in his face. "The horse troubles you," she said, her voice a whisper as she touched his arm.

Paris nodded, his gut churning. "Something's wrong, Helen. I feel it in my bones."

Suddenly, a scream tore through the night. Paris's heart pounded as he grabbed his sword, the polished bronze glinting dangerously. He barked orders for Helen to find Andromache and her son and take the royal tunnel to the barge waiting to evacuate them.

Chaos exploded in the square. The wooden horse splintered open, and Greek soldiers, concealed within, flooded the streets like a tide of death. Paris's worst fears had come true.

"To arms!" he bellowed, his voice slicing through the chaos. "Trojans, to arms!"

The city guards, though taken by surprise, rallied around him. Steel met steel as the Greeks launched their assault. Paris's bow twanged with deadly precision, his arrows felling enemy after enemy with a fury born of desperation.

He pursued the invaders to the gates, knowing they aimed to breach them for the army outside. Sweat and blood mingled on his skin as he reached the heavy gates, his heart thundering.

But he was too late. The gates groaned open, and the Greek army surged in, an unstoppable wave of destruction. Paris's eyes locked on a figure at the front—Odysseus, the architect of this deadly ruse.

With a savage cry, Paris charged. Their swords met with a clash that reverberated through the battlefield. The fight was fierce, each strike a testament to their hatred. But Odysseus was as cunning in combat as he was in strategy.

A sharp pain erupted in Paris's side—Odysseus's blade had found its mark. Paris staggered, his vision blurring as he fell to his knees. Around him, Troy was engulfed in flames, the air thick with the screams of his people.

As darkness closed in, Paris's thoughts drifted to Helen, Andromache, and her son. Had they escaped? The Greeks might take Troy, but they would never erase its legacy.

With his last breath, Paris swore that Troy's fall would only mark the beginning of a legend, one that would resound through the ages.

(507 words)

What makes this work?

This version is a fast-paced thriller set during the fall of Troy, focused on Paris's last stand against the Greeks. It's action-packed and full of tension.

Key Aspects:

- POV: Prince Paris

- Tone: Urgent and intense

- Focus: Battle and personal sacrifice

- Style: Direct, with quick action sequences

Strengths:

- You nailed the tension and pace. It feels like a war movie in ancient times.

- Maybe add a bit more about Paris's internal conflict for extra depth.

- Perfect for readers who love action and heroism.

THANK YOU FOR READING ABOUT GENRE FLASH FICTION

THANK YOU FOR DIVING into the world of genre flash fiction with me.

In this book, we've explored the specific challenges of writing stories where you only have 500 to 1,000 words to capture your reader's imagination. Whether it's the tight twists of thrillers, the heartbeats of romance, the eerie echoes of horror, the boundless realms of science fiction, or the rich tapestries of historical fiction, flash fiction demands precision, creativity, and a mastery of genre.

You've learned to understand the reader's expectations—the common plot lines, the tropes, the reader expectations.

The key to writing good genre flash fiction is to lean in to what the reader knows and loved and then provide a satisfying twist, a finale where your story defies expectations and leaves a lasting impact.

Never forget how powerful, and compelling Genre Flash fiction can be.

In Historical Fiction:

- Captures pivotal moments in time, making the past feel immediate and personal.

- Allows for fresh perspectives on well-known events, giving voice to overlooked figures.

- Distils rich settings and complex eras into poignant, memorable snapshots.

In Romance:

- Delivers intense emotional impact through brief, powerful encounters or revelations.

- Explores the essence of relationships, often focusing on key turning points.

- Creates deep connections between characters in just a few words, leaving readers yearning for more.

In Fantasy:
- Introduces imaginative worlds and magical elements with swift, vivid descriptions.

- Captures epic conflicts and mystical moments in a concise, enchanting narrative.

- Provides a platform for original twists on classic tropes, making the impossible feel real.

In Science Fiction:
- Explores futuristic concepts and technologies with sharp, thought-provoking insights.

- Conveys the vastness of space or the complexity of advanced societies in a tight, engaging format.

- Highlights ethical dilemmas and speculative "what if" scenarios in a way that lingers with readers.

Horror:
- Creates a sense of dread and suspense with minimal exposition, relying on atmosphere and suggestion.

- Unleashes terrifying creatures or psychological horrors in brief, haunting encounters.

- Delivers shocking twists or chilling endings that leave a lasting impression.

Thrillers:
- Builds relentless tension and high-stakes conflict in a compact, adrenaline-fueled

narrative.

- Focuses on intense, life-or-death situations that keep readers on the edge of their seats.

- Delivers swift, surprising twists that upend expectations and drive the story home with impact.

When done well, Genre Flash Fiction is the most compelling and memorable short fiction of all.

Happy writing!

25 FLASH FICTION COMPETITIONS IN THE USA.

FLASH FICTION COMPETITIONS HAVE become increasingly popular over the years as more and more writers explore the unique challenges and opportunities offered by this compressed storytelling form. With strict word limits ranging from a few words to a few hundred, flash fiction allows writers to explore and experiment with different genres and styles in a way that is both challenging and rewarding. And as the popularity of flash fiction grows, so does the number of competitions that offer writers the chance to display their talents and win recognition for their work. Whether you're an experienced writer or new to the craft, there's never been a better time to get involved in the exciting world of flash fiction competitions.

- The Writer's Digest Annual Writing Competition

  - Website: https://www.writersdigest.com/writing-competitions

- The Bath Flash Fiction Award

  - Website: https://bathflashfictionaward.com/

- The WOW! Women On Writing Flash Fiction Contest

  - Website: https://www.wow-womenonwriting.com/contest.php

- The 100 Word Story Flash Fiction Contest

- o Website: http://www.100wordstory.org/

- The Glimmer Train Very Short Fiction Contest

  - o Website: http://www.glimmertrain.com/

- The Press 53 Flash Fiction Contest

  - o Website: http://www.press53.com/

- The NANO Fiction Contest

  - o Website: http://nanofiction.org/

- The Boulevard Short Fiction Contest for Emerging Writers

  - o Website: https://www.boulevardmagazine.org/short-fiction-contest/

- The Blue Mesa Review Flash Fiction Contest

  - o Website: http://bmr.unm.edu/

- The American Short(er) Fiction Contest

  - o Website: https://americanshortfiction.org/

- The Black Warrior Review Fiction Contest

  - o Website: http://bwr.ua.edu/

- The Sonora Review Flash Fiction Contest

  - o Website: http://sonorareview.com/

- The CutBank Literary Magazine Flash Fiction Contest

  - o Website: https://www.cutbankonline.org/

- The Mississippi Review Prize

  - o Website: https://www.mississippireview.com/

- The Baltimore Review Flash Fiction Contest

  - Website: http://baltimorereview.org/

- The Smokelong Quarterly Award for Flash Fiction

  - Website: http://www.smokelong.com/

- The Short Grain Contest (Grain Magazine)

  - Website: https://grainmagazine.ca/

- The New Millennium Writings Award for Fiction

  - Website: https://newmillenniumwritings.org/

- The Prime Number Magazine Awards for Flash Fiction

  - Website: http://www.primenumbermagazine.com/

- The Fish Flash Fiction Prize

  - Website: http://www.fishpublishing.com/

- The CRAFT Flash Fiction Prize

  - Website: https://www.craftliterary.com/

- The Vestal Review VERA Flash Fiction Prize

  - Website: http://www.vestalreview.org/

- The Masters Review Flash Fiction Contest

  - Website: https://mastersreview.com/

- The Carve Magazine Raymond Carver Short Story Contest

  - Website: https://www.carvezine.com/

- The Willow Springs Fiction Prize

- Website: http://willowspringsmagazine.org/

10 FLASH FICTION COMPETITIONS IN THE UK

- **Bath Flash Fiction Award**

  - WEBSITE: HTTPS://BATHFLASHFICTIONAWARD.COM/
    - Offers various prizes including a top prize of£1,000.

- **Fish Publishing Flash Fiction Prize**

  - Website:https://www.fishpublishing.com/flash-fiction-contest-2021/
    - Offers a top prize of €1,000.

- **Reflex Fiction Flash Fiction Competition**

  - https://www.reflexfiction.com/flash-fiction-contest-schedule/
    - Offers a top prize of £1,000.

- **Bridport Prize Flash Fiction Competition**

  - https://www.bridportprize.org.uk/flash-fiction
    - Offers a top prize of £1,000.

- **National Flash Fiction Youth Competition**

  - https://www.nationalflashfictionday.co.uk/competition
    - Offers various prizes for young writers.

- **Farnham Flash Fiction Competition**

  - https://www.farnhamfringefestival.org/farnham_flash-2023.html
    - 3 prizes starting at £75.

- **TSS Flash Fiction Competition**

  - https://www.theshortstory.co.uk/competitions/flash-fiction-400/
    - Offers a top prize of £400.

- **The Fiction Desk Ghost Story Competition**

  - https://www.thefictiondesk.com/submissions/ghost-story-competition.php
    - Offers a top prize of £500.

- **The Mogford Prize for Food and Drink Writing**

  - https://www.mogfordprize.co.uk/flash-fiction-competition
    - Offers a top prize of £10,000.

- **Retreat West Flash Fiction Prize**

  - https://www.retreatwest.co.uk/competitions/flash-fiction-competition/
    - Offers a top prize of £400.

- **Cambridge Short Story Prize Flash FictionCompetition**

  - https://www.cambridgeshortstoryprize.com/flash-fiction
    - Offers a top prize of £100.

Please note that details and deadlines may change, so it's important to visit each competition's website for the most up-to-date information.

20 FLASH FICTION COMPETITIONS IN CANADA

THE NEW QUARTERLY NICK Blatchford Occasional Verse Contest The Writers' Union of Canada Short Prose Competition

- https://www.writersunion.ca/short-prose-competition

PRISM International Creative Non-Fiction Contest

- https://prismmagazine.ca/contests/creative-non-fiction-contest/

Room Magazine Fiction and Poetry Contest

- https://roommagazine.com/contests

Geist Literal Literary Postcard Story Contest

- https://geist.com/postcard-contest

CBC Literary Prizes

- https://www.cbc.ca/books/literaryprizes

Canadian Authors Association Emerging Writer Award

- https://canadianauthors.org/national/emerging-writer-award/

The New Quarterly Edna Staebler Personal Essay Contest

- https://tnq.ca/product/edna-staebler-personal-essay-contest/

Pulp Literature Magazine Raven Short Story Contest

- https://pulpliterature.com/contests/the-raven-short-story-contest/

Antigonish Review Sheldon Currie Fiction Prize
- https://www.antigonishreview.com/index.php

Freefall Literary Society Poetry and Prose Contest
- https://www.freefallmagazine.ca/contest.html

Prairie Fire Press Annual Writing Contests
- https://www.prairiefire.ca/contests/

The Malahat Review Open Season Awards
- https://malahatreview.ca/contests/open_season/info.html

Alberta Views Short Story Contest
- https://albertaviews.ab.ca/contests/

The Peter Hinchcliffe Fiction Award
- https://www.writersunion.ca/peter-hinchcliffe-fiction-award

The Puritan Thomas Morton Memorial Prize
- https://puritan-magazine.com/thomas-morton-memorial-prize/

Windsor Review Short Fiction Contest
- https://windsorreview.wordpress.com/contest-2/

Grain Magazine Short Grain Contest
- https://grainmagazine.ca/short-grain-contest/

The Fiddlehead Literary Journal Short Fiction Contest
- https://thefiddlehead.ca/contest

OVER TO YOU...

CONGRATULATIONS, YOU MADE IT to the end of this book on writing flash fiction! You now have the tools and techniques to craft compelling stories in just a few hundred words. Whether you're an experienced writer looking to hone your skills or a newcomer to the world of writing, flash fiction provides a unique and rewarding way to tell stories.

Remember, writing flash fiction is all about brevity, precision, and impact. Every word count, and every sentence must drive the story forward. But don't let that intimidate you. With practice, you'll find that writing flash fiction can be incredibly freeing and exhilarating. It's a chance to experiment with new ideas and techniques, to push the boundaries of what's possible in storytelling.

And don't forget about the many flash fiction competitions out there. These contests offer a great opportunity to get your work in front of a wider audience, and they can also be a lot of fun. Just remember that winning isn't everything. The real prize is the satisfaction of knowing that you've crafted a story that resonates with readers.

So, keep writing, keep experimenting, and keep pushing yourself to be the best writer you can be. The world needs more great flash fiction, and who knows? Maybe the next great flash fiction story will be yours.

EXTRACT: HOW TO WRITE FLASH FICTION TO WIN COMPETITIONS

SHORT-SHORT STORIES ARE ALL about brevity and concision. Every word counts. You must tell a compelling story in as few words as possible.

Here are my tips:

Start with a Clear Idea

- **Have a clear idea** of your story before you write. You need to know what you want to say and how to say it. **Choose your words wisely.** Stick to the essentials. Don't use unnecessary details. Focus on the main parts of the story: the problem, the characters, and their goals. Make your story tight, no fluff.

- **Use strong and clear language.** Don't be boring. Use words that are descriptive and vivid, that make your reader see and feel things. Use powerful language.

- **Use active voice**. Active voice sentences are more direct than passive voice sentences. Make your writing urgent.

- **Cut extra words.** Get rid of any words or phrases that don't help your story or move it forward. Cut repeated phrases, unnecessary adjectives, and any other words that can be cut without losing the story. Make every word count.

Flash fiction is a unique genre that requires writers to tell a complete narrative in only a couple hundred words. Because of this brevity, finding the right idea is crucial to crafting a successful piece of flash fiction. In this blog, we'll explore some tips for finding and honing your ideas for flash fiction.

Start with an Image or Prompt

One effective approach to find inspiration for flash fiction is to begin with a visual or prompt. This could be anything that sparks your imagination, from a photograph or painting to a simple phrase or word. Let your mind wander and see where the image or prompt takes you. You might be surprised by the story that begins to unfold.

Focus on the Emotions

Another approach to finding an idea for flash fiction is to focus on the emotions you want to convey. What do you want your reader to feel as they read your story?

Use Personal Experience

Drawing from personal experience can be a powerful way to find an idea for flash fiction. Think about a moment in your life that was particularly emotional or impactful.

Refine and Hone Your Idea

Once you have an idea for your flash fiction, it's important to refine and hone it. This means looking for ways to make your story more interesting, engaging, and impactful.

Seek Feedback

Share your work with other writers, friends, or family members and ask for their honest feedback. Consider joining a writing group or workshop, where you can get feedback from other writers and learn from their experiences. Taking in feedback and critiques can help you identify areas where your story could be improved and ultimately help you grow as a writer.

Finding and honing an idea for flash fiction is crucial.

Please take time to look through the suggestions for using Bing AI for generating ideas. Because remember this is what your competition are doing.

Focus on the essentials.

Flash fiction is all about brevity and concision. It's about extracting the key elements of a story and conveying that story in just a few hundred words. But how do you focus on the essentials when writing flash fiction? Here are some tips:

Start with a strong concept.

Flash fiction is all about making an impact in a short amount of time. To do that, you need a strong concept that can be easily expressed in just a few words. Think about what makes your story unique, and how you can capture that in a way that grabs the reader's attention.

Choose your words carefully.

In flash fiction, every word counts. Make sure that each word you use is essential to the story, and that it contributes to the overall impact you're trying to create. Be ruthless in your editing and cut out anything that doesn't add to the story.

Focus on character.

In a short story, character is everything. Focus on creating vivid, memorable characters that the reader can connect with, even in just a few paragraphs. Use details to bring your characters to life and make sure that their motivations and actions are clear and believable.

Incorporate vivid descriptions.

Sensory details can act as a valuable resource in flash fiction, assisting in Think about the sights, sounds, smells, and textures that are essential to your story, and use them to create an image in the reader's mind.

Stick to a single plot.

Flash fiction is not the place for complex plot twists or multiple storylines. Instead, focus on a single plot that can be easily conveyed in a few hundred words. Make sure that the story has a clear beginning, middle, and end, and that the plot is resolved in a satisfying way.

Embrace brevity.

Finally, remember that brevity is the soul of flash fiction. Don't try to cram too much into your story and don't be afraid to leave things unsaid. Sometimes, what you don't say can be just as powerful as what you do say.

Happy writing!

The Unique Twist

Twists can be a powerful tool in flash fiction, helping to keep the reader engaged and creating a sense of surprise and delight. By experimenting with different types of twists and finding the ones that work best for your writing style, you can craft stories that are engaging and memorable, even in just a few hundred words. Here are five story twists that are ideal for flash fiction.

The Unreliable Narrator

One traditional element that can be powerful in flash fiction is the unreliable narrator. This is when the narrator is not telling the truth or is leaving out important information, leading the reader to question the events of the story. Employing this strategy can result in a strong way to cultivate tension and intrigue in a concise setting.

The Unexpected Ending

Another common twist in flash fiction is the unexpected ending. This is when the story ends in a way that the reader did not anticipate, often turning the entire narrative on its head. This can act as a fantastic approach to amaze and please readers, leaving them contemplating the story long after they've finished reading.

The Reversal of Roles

A reversal of roles can be a fun and unexpected twist in flash fiction. This is when the roles of the characters are suddenly reversed, such as the protagonist becoming the antagonist or vice versa. This can generate a feeling of disorientation and surprise that can be effective in a short space.

The Double Twist

A double twist is when the story takes one unexpected turn, only to be followed by another twist that is even more surprising. This can be a demanding technique to execute in short stories, however, when executed effectively, it can leave readers reeling and wanting more.

The Misunderstanding

Finally, the misunderstanding is another classic twist that can be effective in flash fiction. This is when the characters are working from different assumptions or information, leading to a miscommunication that creates conflict and tension. It is an effective method to build suspense and keep the reader engaged in a short space.

The Time Jump

A time jump is when the story suddenly shifts forward or backward in time, often revealing information that shifts the reader's perspective on what has happened so far. This can act as a fantastic approach to keep the reader engaged and create a sense of mystery and intrigue.

The Irony

Irony is when the opposite of what is expected happens, often with humorous or poignant effect. In flash fiction, a well-placed ironic twist can serve as an excellent method to surprise and delight the reader and can be especially effective when used to subvert common tropes or expectations.

The Red Herring

A red herring is a misleading clue or piece of information that is meant to throw the reader off track. In flash fiction, a red herring can be a great way to create tension and misdirect the reader, leading them to a surprising conclusion.

The Revelation

A revelation is when a piece of information is suddenly revealed that changes the reader's understanding of the story. This can be an effective method to generate a sense of surprise and deepen the reader's investment in the characters and the plot.

The Inevitable Conclusion

Finally, the inevitable conclusion is when the reader knows from the beginning of the story how it is going to end but is still drawn in by the journey. This can be a challenge to execute in flash fiction, but when done well, it can create a sense of inevitability and poignancy that lingers long after the story has ended.

Character archetypes that work well in flash fiction

Character archetypes play an essential role in short fiction. These archetypes are universal characters that appear in stories across cultures and time periods. They represent the fundamental aspects of human nature and provide readers with a point of reference when understanding the motives and behaviours of the characters. Whether the protagonist or antagonist, character archetypes can add depth and complexity to a story, allowing readers to relate to the characters and become invested in their journey. By understanding these archetypes, writers can create more dynamic and engaging characters, leading to more captivating and memorable short fiction.

The Outsider: This archetype is often used in flash fiction to create a sense of alienation or detachment from society. The Outsider is typically a character who feels like they don't fit in or belong, and who may be struggling to find their place in the world.

The Rebel: The Rebel is a character who pushes back against authority or the status quo, and who may be seen as a troublemaker or a disruptor. By employing this archetype, tension and conflict can be introduced into a flash fiction story.

The Innocent: The Innocent is a character who is pure of heart and often naïve or inexperienced. This archetype can be employed to generate.

The Hero: The Hero is a classic archetype that can be employed to evoke a sense of bravery, determination, and self-sacrifice. In flash fiction, the Hero may be a character who rises to the challenge in the face of danger or adversity.

The Trickster: The Trickster is a character who delights in playing pranks or pulling off clever schemes. Employing this archetype can be utilized to establish a sense of humor or mischief in a short fictional story.

The Mentor: The Mentor is a character who provides guidance and wisdom to the protagonist. Utilizing this archetype can foster a sense of development or metamorphosis in a flash fiction story, as the protagonist assimilates knowledge from the Mentor's instruction.

The Anti-Hero: The Anti-Hero is a character who may have some heroic qualities, but who is ultimately flawed or morally ambiguous. Employing this archetype can help generate a sense of complexity and nuance in a flash fiction story.

The Lover: The Lover is a character who is driven by passion and emotion. This archetype can be used to create a sense of romance or sensuality in a flash fiction story, or to explore themes of love and desire.

These are just a few examples of character archetypes that can work well in flash fiction. Of course, there are many other archetypes to choose from, and you may find that a different archetype works better for your particular story. The key is to choose an archetype that will help you create a compelling character that resonates with your readers.

Using sensory details in flash fiction

Using sensory details is an effective way to bring your flash fiction to life and immerse your readers in the story. By appealing to the senses, you can create a vivid and memorable reading experience that engages your readers' imaginations. In this blog post, we'll explore the senses that can be used in flash fiction and provide some examples of how to use sensory details effectively.

Sight

Sight is one of the most commonly used senses in fiction, and for good reason. By describing what characters see, you can create a clear picture of the setting, the characters, and the action. For example:

- "The sun was setting over the mountains, casting a warm orange glow across the valley."

- "She wore a bright red coat that stood out against the drab, gray city streets."

Sound

Sound can be used to create a mood and atmosphere in your flash fiction. By describing the sounds that characters hear, you can evoke emotions and set the tone for the story. For example:

- "The wind howled through the empty streets, rattling the windows and sending shivers down their spines."

- "The sound of her laughter echoed through the park, filling the air with joy and energy."

Touch

Describing the way things feel can help to ground your flash fiction in reality and create a sense of physicality. By using tactile language, you can make your readers feel like they are a part of the story. For example:

- "The sand was hot and gritty beneath their feet, sticking to their skin and filling their shoes."

- "Her fingers brushed against the rough bark of the tree as she ran, feeling the roughness against her skin."

Taste

Although taste may not be as commonly used as other senses in flash fiction, it can be an effective way to add depth to your descriptions and create a more immersive reading experience. For example:

- "The warm, buttery croissant melted in her mouth, filling her with a sense of contentment and satisfaction."

- "The bitter taste of coffee filled his mouth, waking him up and giving him the energy to face the day."

Smell

Smell is a powerful sense that can evoke memories and emotions. By describing the scents that character's encounter, you can create a strong sense of atmosphere and mood in your flash fiction. For example:

- "The air was heavy with the scent of jasmine, filling her nostrils with its sweet, heady fragrance."

- "The acrid smell of smoke filled the room, making her eyes water and her throat itch."

Incorporating sensory details into your flash fiction can elevate your writing and make your stories more immersive and engaging. By appealing to your readers' senses, you can create a reading experience that is both memorable and enjoyable. So, the next time you're writing flash fiction, remember to use sensory details to bring your story to life!

Choosing your words carefully in flash fiction

Let's dig deep into what it means to use your words carefully.

Use Strong verbs and active voice. Verbs are the words that show action and emotion. Use strong verbs that say a lot in one word. An active voice to make your story more urgent and real.

- Example, instead of "She was walking slowly," try "She sauntered" or "She limped." These verbs show how she feels and moves.

- Example, instead of "The cake was eaten by the dog," try "The dog devoured the cake."

Cut extra words and filler phrases. Every word counts Every word should help your story and move it forward.

- Example, instead of "She was thinking about what to do next," try "She pondered her next move." This saves words and shows her thoughts better.

- Check for common filler phrases: "in order to," "that," "very," and "just."

Use specific details to create vivid imagery. You don't have space for long descriptions of characters or settings. Instead, use specific details that show the essence of the story. These details can be sensory, like sight, sound, smell, touch, and taste, or emotional, like thoughts or feelings.

- Example, instead of "The house was old," try "The peeling paint on the shutters suggested the house had seen better days." This detail shows the house and the mood better. Specific details can also make your story more vivid and engage your reader's senses.

- Example, instead of "The car crashed," try "The metal crumpled like tin foil, the sound of shattering glass ringing in her ears."

Consider connotation and tone. Connotation is the emotion or culture that a word has, while tone is your attitude toward the story.

Use figurative language to add depth and nuance.

- Example, instead of "He died," try "He passed away," or "He crossed over." See how these words have different emotions and can affect how your reader feels.

- Example, instead of "She cried," try "Tears streamed down her face," or "She wept uncontrollably." These also show different levels of emotion and tone.

Similes, metaphors, and all that... All create vivid imagery and convey complex emotions and ideas. You really want to paint a picture in the reader's mind.

For example, instead of "The sun was hot," try "The sun beat down on her like a hammer." This simile not only describes the heat but also adds a sense of urgency to the story. The comparison to a hammer suggests the relentless and punishing nature of the sun's heat.

Here are some strong verbs:

Love & Romance:
- Adore

- Cherish

- Devote

- Embrace

- Enchant

- Idolize

- Romance

- Treasure

- Worship

Identity & Self Awareness:
- Claim

- Define

- Discover

- Embody

- Express

- Identify

- Project

- Reinvent

- Transform

Social Justice & Advocacy:
- Advocate

- Challenge

- Empower

- Fight

- Oppose

- Protest

- Resist

- Transform

- Unite

Death:

- Depart

- Dissolve

- Emerge

- Exit

- Pass

- Rest

- Surrender

- Transcend

- Vanish

Humour:

- Amuse

- Chuckle

- Entertain

- Jest

- Joke

- Laugh

- Satirize

- Tease

- Wit

Satire:

- Condemn

- Critique

- Lampoon

- Mock

- Parody

- Ridicule

- Satirize

- Scorn

- Spoof

It's important to note that these are just a few examples and there are many other strong verbs that could be used in each theme. When selecting verbs, it's also important to consider the tone and mood of your writing and choose words that align with your intended effect on the reader.

Less is More: Mastering Single-Plot Flash Fiction

While there are many approaches to writing flash fiction, one of the most effective strategies is to focus on a single plot.

Why Single-Plot Flash Fiction Works

At its core, flash fiction is all about distilling a story down to its essential elements. With a primary focus on a single plot, you give your readers a clear and concise narrative that leaves a lasting impact. By eliminating extraneous subplots or tangents, you can create a sense of urgency and immediacy that grabs your reader's attention and holds it until the very end.

Single-plot flash fiction also allows for a greater sense of control over the pacing and structure of your story. By homing in on a specific set of events, you can carefully craft the way in which your story unfolds, building tension and anticipation with each carefully chosen detail.

Tips for Mastering Single-Plot Flash Fiction

If you're new to writing flash fiction, or if you're looking to refine your skills, here are some tips for crafting compelling single-plot stories:

Start with a clear idea: Before you start writing, make sure you have a clear idea of what your story will be about. Choose a single event or situation that you can explore in depth and consider how you want to convey the emotional impact of that event to your reader.

Keep it simple: When it comes to flash fiction, less is definitely more. Avoid overcomplicating your story with too many characters or subplots and focus on creating a single narrative that is both concise and impactful.

Use sensory details: While you may not have a lot of words to work with in flash fiction, you can still create a vivid and immersive world for your reader by using sensory details. Consider how your characters experience the world around them and use descriptive language to bring those experiences to life.

Make every word count: With so few words to work with, it's essential to make every word count. Choose your words carefully and consider how each sentence contributes to the overall impact of your story.

Focus on the ending: In flash fiction, the ending is everything. Make sure that your story builds to a satisfying conclusion that leaves a lasting impression on your reader.

The Benefits of Single-Plot Flash Fiction

Mastering single-plot flash fiction can be a challenging but rewarding experience. By focusing on a single plot, you can create stories that are both concise and impactful, leaving a lasting impression on your readers. Whether you're a seasoned writer or just starting out, honing your skills in single-plot storytelling can help you become a better writer overall, and give you a powerful tool for crafting memorable stories in any genre.

Single-Plots for flash fiction?

Here are just a few examples to get you started with thanks to ChatGPT.

Single plot ideas for flash fiction:

- A character's quest to find a lost object or person.

- A character's struggle to overcome a specific fear or phobia.

- A chance encounter that leads to unexpected consequences.

- A character's decision to take a risk and the outcome of that decision.

- A relationship between two characters that takes a surprising turn.

- A character's attempt to hide a secret or keep a promise.

- A character's realization that they have been living a lie.

- A character's attempt to right a wrong they have committed.

- A character's journey to find closure after a significant event.

- A character's attempt to escape a dangerous or difficult situation.

- A character's attempt to reconnect with a long-lost friend or family member.

- A character's realization that they are stuck in a rut and their journey to break free.

- A character's attempt to make a difficult decision that will impact their future.

- A character's attempt to make amends for past mistakes.

- A character's struggle to forgive someone who has wronged them.

- A character's journey to find their purpose in life.

- A character's attempt to save a failing relationship.

- A character's struggle to come to terms with a terminal illness.

- A character's attempt to uncover the truth about a mysterious event or person.

- A character's realization that their beliefs or values have been challenged and their struggle to come to terms with it.

About Author: Sally Dickson aka Sally Ann Melia

Sally Dickson writes Science Fiction under the pen name

Born in Wallasey, Sally Ann Melia moved to the South of France and the cosmopolitan city-state of Monaco, where she spent her teenage years. As the lone English student in a

French school, Sally spent her time writing stories while her classmates learned English. This sparked a lifelong passion for writing, leading her to pen novels, scripts, stories, and articles.

Her most recent novel is:

'Born of Empire.'

His father was murdered, his brother burnt alive, just 2 days to his 14th when he will inherit the Earth. Time to fight back, before they kill him.

- Teodor, loyal, honest, hardworking yet fearful and plagued by bad dreams. An imperial prince and protector of Earth, he was born after the Dome was built to restore and protect the city of London. He is the last and only heir to two thrones, but only if he survives to age 18. And honestly given the choice, he would spend his days in the stables...

- Guy Erma, driven, determined, yet watchful and not trusting the surrounding adults, he dreams of joining the Dome Militant Space Defense, the protectors of Earth, but his application is flawed his birth was never registered. He does not exist. So what is his future, if he cannot attend school, does not have anywhere to live, and no family to call his own?

When these two boys who were born two days apart come face to face, their lives will change forever.

Also by Sally Ann Melia (Author)

So finally, our communications and technology has advanced sufficiently for Aliens to notice us. The only question is what happens next when the UFOs arrive... A new serial following the adventures of a few space scientists and astrophysics students as they uncover and meet the first alien visitors to Earth.

A fun serial of short stories to read on your journey to work, or at night before sleeping then dreaming of far-flung adventures... If you dream of wandering the Champs-Élysées in Paris in spring, if you can imagine sipping champagne in Raffles in Singapore or the Café de Paris in Monte Carlo or even Tiffany's in New York, then welcome. If you can imagine sharing rice-bowls with Sherpas at the base camp of Everest or watching kangaroo herds race across the outback, then you have come upon kindred spirits. If you'd enjoy taking a medieval chorister's pew to listen to Christmas evensong sung by Oxford's senior choir or sitting on a velvet banquette in Vienna's Opera House to watch Mozart's Marriage of Figaro, please sit back, relax and enjoy.

Join me as we travel from one glittering location to another, we will be aliens, and also meet aliens, as we explore the most exotic streets and savour the greatest wonders of our planet together...

Made in the USA
Columbia, SC
17 December 2024

49772354R00085